Anonymous

**Pictorial Journey through the Holy Land**

Or, Scenes in Palestine

Anonymous

**Pictorial Journey through the Holy Land**
*Or, Scenes in Palestine*

ISBN/EAN: 9783744756365

Printed in Europe, USA, Canada, Australia, Japan

Cover: Foto ©Andreas Hilbeck / pixelio.de

More available books at **www.hansebooks.com**

SHEIKH EID AND SHEIKH 'AISĪ—BEDOWIN CHIEFS OF THE 'ALAWÍN TRIBE.

# PICTORIAL JOURNEY

THROUGH THE

# HOLY LAND;

OR,

## Scenes in Palestine.

MOUNT CARMEL.

LONDON:
THE RELIGIOUS TRACT SOCIETY:
56, PATERNOSTER ROW; 65, ST. PAUL'S CHURCHYARD; AND 164, PICCADILLY.
1863.

## INTRODUCTORY NOTE.

The Illustrations in this Volume present most of the memorable scenes that meet the eye of the traveller in passing through the Holy Land. They are drawn on wood by the author of the letter-press, from sketches taken by him on the spot. The series is extracted from the "Sunday at Home" for 1861.

# CONTENTS.

|  |  | PAGE |
|---|---|---|
| I. | EL ARABAH; OR, THE WILDERNESS OF ZIN | 1 |
| II. | KADESH BARNEA | 7 |
| III. | THE HILL COUNTRY OF JUDEA | 13 |
| IV. | HEBRON | 19 |
| V. | HEBRON—THE OAK OF ABRAHAM | 25 |
| VI. | THE VALLEY OF ESHCOL.—FENCED CITIES OF JUDAH | 31 |
| VII. | ANTIQUITY OF HEBRON.—THE POOLS OF SOLOMON | 37 |
| VIII. | SOLOMON'S WORKS—THE TOWER OF DAVID | 41 |
| IX. | ROUTE FROM HEBRON TO JERUSALEM.—THE POOL OF HEZEKIAH | 45 |
| X. | JERUSALEM—THE TOMBS OF DAVID AND HIS SUCCESSORS—THE "LARGE UPPER ROOM"—VIA DOLOROSA—ARCH OF ECCE HOMO | 51 |
| XI. | GETHSEMANE | 59 |
| XII. | THE VALLEY OF JEHOSHAPHAT | 65 |
| XIII. | CHRISTIAN ANTIQUARIES IN JERUSALEM | 71 |
| XIV. | THE WATERS OF SILOAM AND THE KING'S GARDEN | 75 |
| XV. | THE WATERS OF JERUSALEM | 81 |
| XVI. | THE VALLEY OF THE SON OF HINNOM | 87 |
| XVII. | THE MOUNTAIN OF THE LORD'S HOUSE | 93 |
| XVIII. | EL HARAM ESH-SHERIF, OR THE NOBLE SANCTUARY | 99 |
| XIX. | JERUSALEM AND ITS SIEGES | 105 |
| XX. | THE HOLY SEPULCHRE | 111 |
| XXI. | THE MOUNT OF OLIVES | 115 |
| XXII. | VIEW FROM OLIVET | 119 |
| XXIII. | "THE TOWN OF MARY AND HER SISTER MARTHA" | 123 |
| XXIV. | JERUSALEM AND ITS INHABITANTS | 127 |
| XXV. | "BETHLEHEM AND THE LAND OF JUDAH." | 131 |
| XXVI. | THE CONVENTS IN THE LAND OF JUDAH | 137 |
| XXVII. | DESCENT TO JERICHO AND THE DEAD SEA | 141 |
| XXVIII. | THE ACCURSED SEA AND THE SACRED RIVER | 145 |
| XXIX. | JERICHO AND THE CITIES OF THE PLAIN | 151 |
| XXX. | PISGAH AND GILGAL | 155 |
| XXXI. | JERICHO AND BETHEL | 161 |
| XXXII. | FROM JERICHO TO SHECHEM | 165 |
| XXXIII. | THE MOUNTAIN OF BLESSING | 171 |
| XXXIV. | SYCHAR TO SAMARIA | 177 |
| XXXV. | FROM SAMARIA TO EN-GANNIM | 183 |
| XXXVI. | THE GREAT PLAIN AND JEZREEL | 189 |
| XXXVII. | FROM JEZREEL TO TIBERIAS | 195 |
| XXXVIII. | GALILEE OF THE GENTILES | 201 |

# SCENES IN PALESTINE.

## I.

## EL ARABAH; OR, THE WILDERNESS OF ZIN.

ONE land, and one alone, possesses an absorbing interest for those people of all races, in all parts of the world, who profess the name of Christ. No matter how much their one common tenet of faith in the Redeemer may be obscured by prejudice, or encumbered by superstition, if they believe in Christ at all, their attention will be at once attracted by anything which relates to the land in which the whole natural mortal life of him, who put on our flesh and dwelt among us, was passed. Year by year, as that land and the districts adjacent to it are further explored, some fresh facts are ever being added to our still imperfect information concerning the localities mentioned in the Bible. Deeply interesting must it be to any Christian to wander throughout the country which was the subject of God's gracious promise to his chosen people. Still more interesting is it to him to see that each new discovery, geographical or archæological, however trifling in itself, which it may be his privilege to make, acquires a value altogether disproportionate to its own magnitude, because it bears upon a subject of such vital importance to us all, namely, the truth of every jot and every tittle of God's revealed word. Every such discovery will, he finds, corroborate some assertion, explain some allusion, or show the fulfilment of some prophecy contained in that book, which we have humbly received as written under the direct inspiration of the Holy Spirit; and thus one more link is added to the long chain of indubitable facts, which proves to us that our faith in the word of God is not credulity, and our trust in the promises of Scripture is not a vain dream.

The traveller approaching Palestine from the south, cannot fail to see how literal is the fulfilment of the denunciations against Edom which God put into the mouths of his holy prophets. He beholds Edom, who dwelt " in the clefts of the rock and held the height of the hill," who made her " nest as high as the eagle "—now " a desolate wilderness;" that her cities lie waste, that she is " most desolate," and that her cities do not return. God has indeed, according

B

to his word, "laid the mountains of Esau and his heritage waste for the dragons of the wilderness."

It is from Edom's rock-hewn capital that the frontier of Judea is approached. A deep mountain basin is strewed with Petra's ruins, is hemmed around by a perpendicular wall of cliffs, whose precipices are sculptured for the façades and excavated for the chambers, which served the indwellers of this "nest in the rock" for habitations during life, for temples in which to worship, and for tombs where all that was mortal of them at last was laid. The descent northwards is through a series of ravines that often are mere rifts in the mountain—channels by which the waters of winter's storms rush down to the plain.

One great valley, beginning almost as far north as Mount Hermon, runs from north to south through Southern Syria, and continues its course still further to the southward. Its upper portion is the valley of the Jordan, commonly called by Arabs "El Ghor." By most of the Arabian geographers this name is applied to the valley of the Jordan exclusively; but one of them, Abulfelda, says that the Ghor extends continuously to the Red Sea from the Lake of Tiberias. The ancient geographers are silent as to the prolongation of the great valley from the Dead Sea to the Red Sea. The central portion of the valley is occupied by the Dead Sea in its greatest length, and by a small tract at its southern extremity, which is "the Valley of Salt" of the Scriptures, reaching up to some declivities that are probably those called in the Bible "the ascent of Akrabbim." From these cliffs the great plain to which the name "El Arabah" is given by the Arabs, and which was wholly unknown to the last generation of travellers, commences, and continues uninterruptedly to the site of ancient Elath, at the head of the Gulf of Akabah on the Red Sea.

Burckhardt, in 1812, was the first to visit and describe this great valley as it exists, and it was not till 1822 that his full description was published; but the first two travellers who passed down its whole length from sea to sea, were M. de Bertou and Dr. Robinson, within a few weeks of each other, in the year 1838.

"El Arabah," or "Wady Arabah" of the modern Arabs, is a broad valley or plain of rolling gravelly desert, commencing at the cliffs which terminate the "Valley of Salt," which was called by the Crusaders the "Vallis Illustris," and running southward between the granite peaks and weatherworn sandstone ranges of Edom on the east, and the steep limestone ridges of the south-eastern boundary of the land of Judah on the west; which ridges, continued further south, divide the Arabah from the great desert of Et Tih, and then terminates at the shore of the Red Sea.

MOUNTAINS OF EDOM, AND THE WILDERNESS OF ZIN.

Unlike most of the Arabian wadys or valleys, the Arabah is almost destitute of any scenery that is strikingly picturesque. It is singularly bleak, barren, and desolate, and very subject to sandstorms. The centre of the valley is almost devoid of vegetable life; but over the southern portion, and in the wadys that descend to it from the mountains, plants occur in larger and more frequent patches. The breadth of the valley varies, but it probably does not often exceed ten or twelve miles, and the greater part of it is of a less width.

This dreary waste, that seems so wearisome and uninteresting in its whole extent, from the southern extremity of the Dead Sea down to the site of ancient Elath at the head of the Gulf of Akabah in the Red Sea, is replete with interest, and very rich in association for the Bible student. The Israelites probably journeyed up it northwards on their road to Kadesh Barnea, and they assuredly passed down it southwards when Edom had refused them a passage through his land.

This gloomy wilderness has been the scene of many manifestations of God's almighty power that were directly miraculous—altogether out of the common course of natural events; for in it, or in its immediate neighbourhood, occurred some of the most remarkable episodes connected with the forty years' probation of the people of Israel.

El Arabah was "the wilderness of Zin." On the north it saw the smoke ascending to heaven from the dire catastrophe that befell the cities of the plain; Elath and Hazeroth were in its southern border, Meribah Kadesh was within its limits, and Mount Hor looked down on a great part of its extent.

When the geographical features of the Arabah were first made known, it was supposed that it had once formed part of the valley of the Jordan, and that the river flowing down it originally emptied itself into the Red Sea. It was also believed that, but for the wonderful depression of the basin of the Dead Sea, the Jordan would now flow through the Arabah from north to south. The present level of the region, however, is opposed to these views, for it has been ascertained that the Arabah, for at least two-thirds of its length, and probably for a still greater proportion, slopes down northwards to the Dead Sea. The watershed is somewhere south of the southern Wady Ghurundel, but its exact position has not yet been determined.

Since this discovery it has been suggested that, in the convulsion by which Sodom and Gomorrah were destroyed, the level of the northern part of the Arabah was changed, and that it then sank down into its present abnormal position.

The name Arabah is now limited to the plain south of the Dead Sea. In the Hebrew Bible, however, a knowledge of the existence of the Arabah, and of its name, is very early found. The book of Deuteronomy opens thus: "These be the words which Moses spake unto all Israel on this side Jordan, in the wilderness, in the plain over against the Red Sea, between Paran, and Tophel, and Laban, and Hazeroth, and Dizahab." The plain here mentioned is in Hebrew, "Arabah," and corresponds in reality as well as in name with the great valley that has been just described. The Hebrew word "Arabah," which when used generally means a desert plain, is here applied with the article, *the* Arabah, as the proper name of the great valley in question, in its whole length, just as the name applied to the southern portion is used in the same form, as a proper name, in Arabic. In Scripture, the Dead Sea is even called "the Sea of the Arabah, the Salt Sea;" and the Arabah of the Hebrews, therefore, like the "Ghor" of Abulfelda, was the great valley in its whole extent, from Tiberias to the Red Sea; so that when the Israelites were in the plains of Moab, opposite Jericho, they are spoken of as being in the Arabah "over against the Red Sea," that is, opposite to the Red Sea, or in the further part of the plain from that sea; Tophel (the modern Tufileh) being east of the plain just south of the Dead Sea, and the wilderness of Paran to the south-west. Thus, in our present state of knowledge respecting the Arabah, the Scriptures receive an important illustration in some passages, which, before this country had been properly explored, could not be satisfactorily explained.

In this plain, this great valley—the "Arabah" of the Bible, the "Ghor" of Abulfelda—it was, that Moses, at the end of the fortieth year of Israel's punishment in the desert, recapitulated to them the wonderful tale of God's long-suffering mercy, of the marvels he had wrought on their behalf, of their frequent rebellion against him, and of the penalties which, though he was slow to anger, they had drawn down upon themselves. He set forth all God's gracious promises to them; and then, having set before them "life and good, and death and evil," he adjured them to obey the Lord who had done so much for them by signs, and wonders, and a mighty hand, and a stretched-out arm.

## II.

## KADESH BARNEA.

Leaving the mountains of Edom, and entering into the Arabah, the plain is found to be about eleven or twelve miles broad. A ride of six hours over the level desert, thickly studded with mimosas and tamarisks, brings the traveller to the fountains called "Ain Weibeh," on the first slope of the limestone hills which bound the Arabah to the westward. Here are three pools, a few rods apart, supplied by springs issuing from the chalky rock, and partly surrounded by a swamp and thick jungle of tall reeds, coarse grass, and wild palms. From the midst of this rank vegetation rises a graceful group of palm trees, crowned with leafy tresses in all their rich natural luxuriance, untrimmed and untouched by the hand of man.

The pools are edged with blackish mud, and the water they contain is covered with scum at the brink, and emits a strong sulphureous smell. This turbid liquid is brackish to the taste; but, uninviting as it seems, both the Arabs and their camels drink it eagerly, and the former usually fill their water-skins. Ain Weibeh is a fountain too much frequented by thirsty men and animals for its waters to have much chance of growing clear and pellucid; but though they are far from tempting, the whole scene around the springs is replete with picturesque effect. Groups of men and camels give life to the bare rocky foreground, which slopes down to the water's edge, whilst beyond the still pool the exuberant vegetation of the cane and palm thicket glows with powerful colour, and reeds, and grass, and palms are reflected in the dark waters. Above the line of jungle there is a wide prospect of the Arabah, which, when looked down upon in this manner, seems quite level; and beyond the plain is seen its mountain boundary, while the peak of Mount Hor appears towering above the nearer range.

The whole scene has a kind of wild, strange beauty, though it is rather of a solemn and gloomy character; but there is an interest attaching to this spot far different from, and of far greater moment than, that of any mere material beauty with which nature has endowed it. We have every reason for believing that this now deserted fountain is the site of Kadesh Barnea, the city in Edom's uttermost border mentioned very early in the Old Testament history, before Israel's birth, but chiefly interesting from its very intimate connexion with the wanderings of the Israelites several centuries later.

There is no doubt that after Sinai, the "Mount of God," and the awe-inspiring events that there occurred, the place of all others that arrests our attention in the Bible narrative of the forty years' probation undergone by the stiff-necked children of Israel in the wilderness, is Kadesh Barnea. It was, unquestionably, the most important and interesting of all the Israelites' resting-places mentioned in the itinerary of the book of Numbers, for it was the scene of more of the Almighty's direct interventions in human affairs than any other of the localities enumerated. It is the only place that is called "a city;" and when the Lord's people had at last passed over Jordan into the promised land, it became one of the landmarks by which the boundary of the country given to them by Jehovah was defined. As early as the fourteenth chapter of Genesis, we find mention of "En Mishpat, which is Kadesh," under the following circumstances.

Nearly four thousand years ago, four kings or sheikhs of powerful tribes, from Mesopotamia and Eastern Arabia, made a foray along the east of the Jordan valley, to take vengeance upon some tribes that refused tribute. This was just such an expedition as might have taken place at any period from that distant epoch down to the present time, if four great chiefs of wandering tribes made a league to ravage the villages of tribes who suddenly abstained from paying the customary black mail to secure their being left to themselves. These four kings then smote the Horites in Mount Seir, made an incursion into the wilderness of Paran, and then wheeled back to "En Mishpat" (the fountain of Mishpat) "which is Kadesh." They then marched northwards, and defeated in battle five kings or sheikhs of the district west of the Dead Sea, and plundered their cities, carrying off Lot, with his family and property, from Sodom.

Abraham, who was encamped near Hebron, heard of his nephew's misadventure, and taking with him three hundred and eighteen "trained servants, born in his house," and his allies, the three brothers, Aner, Eshcol, and Mamre, he pursued the marauders, surprised them by night, and followed them almost as far as Damascus. He rescued Lot, with his property; and it was on his triumphant return from this expedition that he was met by Melchizedek, king of Salem (supposed to be the place afterwards called Jerusalem), priest of the most high God. The king-priest blessed Abraham in God's name, and then blessed God for what he had done for Abraham; after which these two righteous men— one the friend of God, and the other the type of Christ—parted and went their

FOUNTAINS OF AIN WEIBEH, THE SUPPOSED SITE OF KADESH BARNEA.

way. Lot, who had chosen his habitation amongst the wicked, for the sake of worldly gain, received back his family and his goods from his holier relative, and returned to the cities of the plain.

This account of the warfare of the four kings with five proves that Kadesh was a well-known watering-place, even at that very early epoch of the world's history, and it also gives us a general notion of its situation.

The next mention of Kadesh is in the book of Numbers, in connexion with the commencement of the wanderings of the Israelites in the desert. It was here that the whole congregation awaited the return of the spies who had been sent by Moses to survey the land of promise; and hither the twelve spies, who were all chiefs of the people, came back, after having searched the country for forty days.

Caleb and Joshua had a living active faith in God's promises, in his power, and in his will to perform them. The companions of Caleb and Joshua were of another spirit. They mistrusted God, they slandered the land promised to their fathers, and died by the plague of God for their evil and false report. The Israelites sided with the faithless majority, believed their calumnies, murmured against the Lord, and feared the people of the land. Then it was that, on this spot, "the glory of the Lord appeared in the tabernacle of the congregation, before all the children of Israel," and the dread sentence was pronounced which adjudged the whole congregation to a forty years' sojourn in the wilderness.

The God of hosts, however, in judgment remembered mercy, and did not forget those who relied upon his word, for Caleb and Joshua were specially exempted from the fearful condemnation.

To Kadesh Barnea, many long years afterwards, Israel again returned. The wayfarers had now been wasted away by eight and thirty years of pilgrimage. Most of those who in the prime of life had marched up the Arabah when they first sojourned at this spot, slept now in their desert graves, in accordance with God's righteous judgment; and those who were then in the first flush of youthful vigour had now attained middle age, and were worn with travel and hardship.

Now, at Kadesh, Miriam died and was buried; and here, when the fountain failed to supply the vast host encamped around it, Israel, as of yore, murmured and rebelled, and Israel's stubborn mistrust of God's careful protection provoked Moses and Aaron to impatience and disobedience. The two chiefs exclaimed, "Hear now, ye rebels, must *we* fetch you water out of this rock?" They did not attribute power to God, or give him the glory of the miracle that was to follow; and then Moses, in impetuous anger, smote the rock twice, instead of, as he was directed, speaking to it before the eyes of the people. God honoured his old prophet in the people's eyes, and the rock gave forth water for the people's wants; but this momentary presumption of Moses and Aaron lost them the privilege of leading Israel into the land which for so many centuries had been theirs, by Jehovah's faithful promise.

From the time of this fresh outburst of Israel's unbelief, Kadesh acquires an additional appellation, and it was from "the waters of strife," "Meribah Kadesh," that Moses sent messengers to the king of Edom, with an earnest entreaty to be permitted to pass through his land, "by the king's highway." This liberty of passage through Edom was of great importance to Moses and his people, for they had to pass through the land of Moab on their way to the eastern bank of the Jordan, from which they were to cross over to their destined inheritance. Their nearest and easiest road was through one of the valleys leading from the Arabah up to the table-lands of Mount Seir, whence they could at once descend to the plains of Moab on the east of the Dead Sea. But the descendant of Esau fiercely refused to give his kinsman, the progeny of Jacob, a passage through his border, and came out against him with much people and with a strong hand. By God's command Moses retraced his steps to the Red Sea; but before he turned southwards, it was God's will that a portion of the sentence passed upon Moses and Aaron at the waters of strife should be carried out.

Israel journeyed from Kadesh to Mount Hor, on whose summit Aaron died. The congregation then travelled down the Arabah to the Red Sea, in order to compass the land of Edom eastward by a long circuit; and in the rugged defiles between these granite precipices, well might " the soul of the people be much discouraged because of the way."

## III.

## THE HILL COUNTRY OF JUDEA.

From Ain Weibeh the route by which to enter the hill country of Judea is over the mountains of Edom. The first halting place is the fountain of Mureidah, or Magreira, in the wady of the same name, a pool of very bad brackish water, in a brake of canes, rushes, and coarse grass. In this respect it is like Ain Weibeh, but it lacks the beautiful palms, the wide-spread prospect, the solemn beauty, and, what was far beyond all these, the enthralling recollections of the hoary past. The eye rests for a moment upon the patch of refreshing green amidst the glare of the white and yellow slopes around it, but no associations of old times attach to that desert fountain.

A long and steep ascent has then to be mounted to a tract of undulating table-land, of similar character to the rest of the plain, but of a higher elevation. This is crossed until a valley is reached, partly surrounded by a regular and singular amphitheatre of precipitous rocks. Before this there is seen on the left the curious isolated mountain of Madurah, with its flattened summit seemingly crowned by a great fortress. On the top of this mountain, an Arab legend tells us, once stood the city of Madurah. Its inhabitants provoked God to anger, and he in his vengeance destroyed the city with stones from heaven, and turned the dead bodies of the erring people into stones. Seetzen, the traveller, heard this tale at Hebron in the year A.D. 1807, and hoping to find something which might illustrate the account of Lot's wife being turned into a pillar of salt, he made an expedition to the spot, ascended, and carefully examined the mountain. He found no trace of any ruins; and, instead of the petrified corpses of the inhabitants, the small level on the mountain's top was covered with stones, composed of limestone mixed with sand, about the size of a man's head, and of various shapes.

The valley is at the foot of the mountain wall, a ridge of bare limestone at least a thousand feet high, and running north and south, which formed a natural boundary between Judah and Edom. Away to the southward this barrier is less formidable, for it is not so steep or lofty, but to the north there are but three passes into Judah. Two of these, Es Sufah and Es Sufey, are near together, and go straight over the crest of the mountain. The other, which has the credit of being the easiest, lies some distance to the left or to the south-west. It is called El Yemen, and is the only natural break in the great chain. Wady el Yemen is a deep semicircular gash which has cleft the mountain almost to its base, and, according to Seetzen's account, even this pass is not particularly easy or attractive. He describes it as a frightfully wild deep desert gorge, so thickly strewn with huge rocks that it is difficult to find a passage betwixt them.

The shortest route, which crosses the tremendous pass of Es Sufah, is almost straight up the bare surface of the limestone rock. The strata, too, render the ascent more difficult, for they lie at an oblique angle, so that gravity acts on the traveller in two directions at once—one pulling him backwards, the other drawing him sideways. The rock also is in many places highly polished, partly by the traffic which has passed over it for centuries, but chiefly by the sand ever blown over its superficies in storms. Up this smooth slippery plane travellers scramble as best they may, sometimes right up the steep hill face, sometimes dodging about in zigzag fashion, according as small inequalities in the rock, or any slight roughness of its surface, give some sort of secure holding-ground for the feet, and a means of avoiding the spots most abounding in treacherous glaze. The pass gives plentiful indications that it has been used from a very high antiquity, both in its well-worn road and in the steps hewn in some places, and the narrow paths cut across the slant of the strata in others, many, many centuries ago. The steepness, the smoothness, and the lateral inclination continue up to the summit; and when first standing on the naked plane of rock, it seems almost impossible that any heavily laden beast could ascend the declivity. The broad, flat, spongy feet of the camel, however, are marvellously adapted for such a path, as they do not slip on any dry surface, however polished. On wet ground the case is very different.

The Arabic word "Es Sufah" (a rock) is identical with the Hebrew "Zephath," the same place as "Hormah," which was one of "the uttermost cities of the tribe of the children of Judah towards the coast of Edom southward." It is probable, therefore, that this pass was "the way of the spies," and also the track by which the presumptuous Israelites endeavoured to enter Palestine contrary to the commands of God, in which attempt they were routed and driven back by king Arad the Canaanite. Israel then was in the commission of an act of sin; and their sin, by God's permission, caused their punishment. Afterwards, when they visited Kadesh a second time, king Arad fought against them unprovoked, and took some of them prisoners. The Almighty would not suffer a heathen chieftain to work evil to his chosen people without his special

THE HILL COUNTRY OF JUDEA.

permission. The Israelites on this occasion were acting in accordance with God's commands; and when they prayed for retribution on their assailant, their prayer was heard, and the Canaanites and their cities were doomed to destruction. No site of a city has been discovered in this wild region, which is not surprising, for the last mention of Hormah is in the reign of David. Near the foot of the pass is a ruined tower, evidently intended to guard its approach. On two of the hills also, after crossing the top of the range, ruined towers of good masonry are seen; and across a valley leading down from one of them is a substantial dam, built of cut stone, showing that some cultivation anciently was carried on in this now desert spot.

From the crest of Es Sufah a parting view may be taken of the Arabah, before descending to Wady Teraibeh. The descent is comparatively short and easy, for on this northern side of the ridge the country is a table-land far above the level of the Arabah.

On a rise near at hand is a burying-place, the graves being marked by upright stones, upon many of which, strange to say, rude crosses were cut. A few have the addition of two upright strokes beside the cross. It is difficult to account for the origin of these crosses, for the whole population of the wild country on both sides of the barrier is Moslem, and the stones have no appearance of great antiquity. Curiously enough, Captains Irby and Mangles observed crosses scrawled about the door of a Turkish edifice near Kerak (the "Kir Moab" of Scripture) on the east of the Dead Sea, and also these signs " + λ7," were three times repeated there, but they give no guess as to their authors. Some of the Bedouin tribes adjoining the Arabah occasionally kill a kid or a lamb as a sacrifice to secure a prosperous journey, and to preserve the lives of their camels, on whose necks they smear crosses with the blood of the victim. This sign may be used in this case in thoughtless imitation of the monks at Sinai, or perhaps merely as a simple mark. They certainly would not sculpture crosses on stone. Some of the Moslem tribes of Northern Africa, the Kabyles of the Atlas for instance, tattoo the sign of the cross upon their foreheads. Why they do so has not been satisfactorily explained; but their tombs never bear this sacred symbol. It seems improbable that any travellers casually encamped near this place of Moslem sepulture would engrave crosses upon Arab tombs.

Hormah is within the confines of Palestine, in "the south country," the land of the Lion of Judah, the country allotted to the children of Simeon; for "their inheritance was within the inheritance of the children of Judah," and "the part of the children of Judah was too much for them." Their inheritance was given to them by lot, and then they had to win it. But they had a powerful ally, for "the Lord was with them," and over this immediate neighbourhood the sword of Judah and Simeon passed. "They slew the Canaanites that inhabited Zephath, and utterly destroyed it; and the name of the city was called Hormah."

Passing onwards into the hill country of Judah, the traveller is now truly in a Bible land. It was a wild frontier district, and was given to the fierce and valiant tribes of Judah and Simeon, who could guard it well. On its swelling hills are still scattered the relics of its "fenced cities," and many a height is crowned by the ruin of some strong fort or massive tower. For their history we must turn to Scripture; and, with few exceptions, in Scripture alone do we find the names so familiar to all who have been educated in a free and Protestant land, where those who will can study God's holy word. All that interests us in this district is of a sacred character, and finds no place in secular history. It does not present, as the Arabah does, any striking geographical or geological features for study or speculation. Its downs are hardly as picturesque as their fellows in England. The relics of old days are far from imposing, and the physical aspect of the land is dull and monotonous. Viewed simply as it is materially, and putting aside its religious associations, to travel through it would be very tiresome, and a narration of the journey would be wearisome. But the Christian pilgrim, who views the land through the light of God's word, feels it a privilege to tread this sacred soil, and carries in his breast recollections that beguile the tedium, and holy thoughts that cause him to forget the fatigues of his way; while the Christian, whose lot is cast so that he can only be a pilgrim in spirit, and not in the flesh, will feel his heart warm, and his attention kindle at the plainest, simplest description of the Holy Land. In this pastoral tract, Abraham's flocks pastured, and David tended sheep. Here Elijah wandered; here Ruth gleaned; here angels walked; and here He, who was "the root and the offspring of David, and the bright and morning star," came into this world of sin for its salvation.

## IV.

## HEBRON.

So many of the most remarkable events in the history of the patriarchs took place in the Land of the tribe of Judah, and it is so closely connected both with the record of the early days of Israel's possession of Canaan, and with the biography of David, that we must dwell somewhat more in detail on its general features, and on some of its most familiar sites.

The land which fell by lot to the sons of Judah was bounded on the east by the whole length of "the Salt Sea," from the mouth of the Jordan to the Valley of Salt. From thence their frontier took a south-westerly direction: skirting the territory of Edom, passing by Kadesh, and afterwards turning to the north-west, it struck the coast of the Mediterranean somewhere south of Gaza. The Mediterranean was its western limit, whilst on the north its boundary ran from the mouth of the Jordan somewhat northwards, and then along the south brow of the Vale of Hinnom; thence going directly westward, it passed through "Ain Esh Shems" (the Scripture "Bethshemesh") and Tibneh (Timnath): it then turned northwards to Akir (Ekron), and went out from thence to the sea coast.

The tribe of Simeon was scattered through this district; and the wild Bedouin children of the Kenite, Moses' father-in-law, who had cast in their lot with Israel, also chose to wander forth with an ancestral instinct into the savage wilderness of Judah, south of Arad, on the skirts of the Dead Sea, and to dwell there.

The royal cities of Philistia were included in this territory given to Judah, and one by one they fell before Joshua "and all Israel with him;" but the whole of the fertile country along the sea coast, and these great cities themselves, were soon recovered by their former possessors, so that Judah on this side was shut in from all intercourse with foreign nations. Israel was shut out from the sea by the Phœnicians; but to Judah, the Dead Sea was a barrier against eastern nations. The wilderness of Zin, and the wilderness of Tih intervened between them and Egypt, whilst the great fenced cities of Philistia and the iron chariots of their hereditary foes the pagan Philistines effectually debarred them from access to the sea coast.

On entering "the south country," within the limits of the land of promise, there are soon seen slight indications of a change in the character of the country even before crossing the pass of Es Sufah, for every now and then some bright flower enlivens the grim desert. Proceeding onwards, the plants begin to be more plentiful, the flowers appear in more frequent patches; grass too, in isolated tufts, shows itself here and there, herbs increase, shrubs disappear; and slowly and gradually, very gradually in the gravelly valleys, one comes upon pasturage, thin and scattered, but sufficient for considerable flocks. Still the gradations between the great and terrible wilderness, and the land flowing with milk and honey, are almost imperceptible; and there is no spot where any abrupt transition can be marked so as to fix the boundary of the desert and the frontier line of fertility.

Aged Israel in his last hours foretold what would be the position held by the posterity of each of his sons, when they should succeed to their heritage in Canaan. The anger of Simeon and Levi had been fierce, their wrath had been cruel, and God through Israel's mouth pronounced their eventual destiny: "I will divide them in Jacob, and scatter them in Israel." Thus they never could be great or powerful, or rise into importance as a single state; and most literally was this prophecy fulfilled. They had no tract of country allotted to them: they had no border. Cities were given to Simeon here and there, scattered about through Judah's wide inheritance, and to Levi they were assigned in the portion of each of the tribes. The race of Simeon inherited the fierceness of their ancestor, and bore his punishment. The prophetic doom of Levi was literally carried out; but the Almighty's merciful approval of their conduct at Sinai turned the punishment into a blessing. Levi was "scattered in Israel," but it was as the consecrated priests of the Most High, appointed to perform the rites and ceremonies appertaining to his worship.

After ascending a rocky pass out of the valley, somewhat off the road are the ruins of Kurnub, supposed by some to be the "Tamar" mentioned in Ezekiel in connexion with Kadesh, and later the Thamara of Ptolemy. The remains are scattered over some low hills, surrounded by a wall. There are relics of a strong fort, near which is a great underground vault, partly cut out of the rock, with an opening in the top. Further on is an edifice, which contains a large apartment with a bow at the south end, and surrounded by fragments of columns, cornices, capitals, etc. This may have been a Christian church, for some of the ancient churches in this country were built north and south, instead of east

HEBRON.

and west, as in more modern days. A deep ravine ran along one side of the city; and across the valley between two hills, on which are the remains of towers, is a solid dam of masonry.

Bedouin encampments are here met with; their black tents, woven from camels' hair being pitched in a great circle; and their flocks scattered over the fat pasturages, or crowding round some well which a patriarch may have dug, patiently waiting for the water to be drawn up to supply them each in turn. Abraham looked upon just such groups as these in this very land nearly forty centuries ago.

Advancing into the heart of the hill country of Judah, the swelling downs and smooth rounded hills are somewhat bare of herbage; but in the valleys the grass, high and green and luxuriant, is spangled with countless flowers—red anemones, the scarlet poppy, called in Arabic "abou naum," "the father of sleep," mallows, and delicate sweet-scented convolvuli, with many others. Numbers of storks are seen marching solemnly about whilst they feed, but they are shy of allowing too close an approach. Now and then, too, a patch of corn land is passed. Ruined towers often crown the hills, and there are many remains of walls and foundations. There is another change, however, in the aspect of the country, which is not an improvement. It is utterly devoid of trees; there is not even a shrub. The palms of Kadesh, the acacias of the Arabah, the desert broom, the tamarisk, and other smaller plants, have all disappeared, and there is nothing to take their place. At midday, in all "the south country," from the border up to Hebron, there is no such thing as shade.

Leaving on the left the tanks and ruins of Ararah, the Scripture "Aroer," are seen the extensive remains of another ancient city, now called El Milh. This was the Moladah of Scripture, a city on the southern border towards Edom, assigned to Judah, and afterwards made over to Simeon. In later days it was a castle of the Idumeans, mentioned by Josephus as "Malatha;" and afterwards under the Romans it was the station of a cohort.

Near the ruins are some interesting wells of great antiquity. They are deep, their sides are lined with cut stone, and the great blocks of marble at their mouths are seamed with deep grooves all round their edges, worn by the ropes let down to draw the water for many and many a generation. Round the wells a number of troughs, shaped something like mortars, and cut out from blocks of stone or marble of various kinds, are strewed about for the purpose of watering the flocks. This group of wells of good pure water must have been a rich possession in this dry and thirsty land. These at Moladah are almost, without doubt, as old as the patriarchs; and as we look upon the countless furrows on their marble margins, and down into the still cool waters beneath, and then cast our eyes upon the thirsting flocks collected around and upon the bare, hot, gray hills behind them, we can understand how it was that such prominence was given to wells in the Bible, and how often they are inseparably linked with events of the highest importance. The thoughts recur to Achsah, daughter of the God-fearing Caleb, promised by her father as a prize to him who should smite Kirjath-Sepher and take it. Her valiant cousin Othniel won the city and the reward, and then the bride asked a dowry from her father: "Give me a blessing; for thou hast given me a south land; give me also springs of water: and Caleb gave her the upper springs and the nether springs."

Not far from Hebron lies Tell el Kuseifeh, a hill crowned with extensive ruins of a town, where one column of some public building still stands erect among its prostrate fellows. This is one of the many fenced cities of Judah whose names are unknown. About an hour's distance off, is another hill still called Tell Arad, where stood the city Arad, whose king twice wrought evil to Israel, and which afterwards was captured and destroyed by Joshua when he took "the south country."

The valleys through which the traveller now passes are mostly cultivated with corn in the untidy way which is universal among the agricultural Arabs; large patches of coarse grass and weeds being left amidst the corn for no reason whatever. This style of farming answers well enough where there is no stint of land, and a hundred acres more or less are of no account at all to the tribe which owns the country, whilst these rough spots help to give brightness to the scene, for they sparkle with radiant flowers. Quails spring with a quick whirr out of the weeds and corn as one rides onwards; wells and Bedouin encampments, and flocks of sheep and goats, are more frequent. Cattle and horses, too, are now met with; towers, foundations, and other remains of old days crown the hills, and occasionally the dams for vast reservoirs cross the valleys.

At length a view of Hebron is caught from the brow of a hill; and descending its slope, the city of the patriarchs stands on a bare hill face, glittering in the sunshine. Beneath it lies a fair fresh valley wooded with olive-groves, which also cover the terraces of the opposite hill. The houses, many of which have semicircular domes rising from their flat roofs, climb the steep, tier over tier; and above them, like a giant among dwarfs, towers the mighty mosque which covers the cave of Machpelah. Here Abraham first buried his dead out of his sight, and afterwards was himself entombed; here Isaac and Rebecca rest; here Leah, the tender-eyed and unloved, sleeps in peace; and here, after a long circuitous journey out of Egypt, the embalmed corpse of Jacob was at last laid.

## V.

## HEBRON—THE OAK OF ABRAHAM.

On approaching *Hebron*, the city of the patriarchs presents itself as a bright cheerful town, clinging to the steep hill-face on one side of the famed and fertile vale, plenteously enriched with shade, forming a landscape which contrasts strongly with that upon which the traveller from the south has looked for many days.

The southern approach to Hebron—"the way of the spies"—would be attractive if the scene possessed nothing but its own physical beauty and freshness to recommend it; but this earthly comeliness is its least attraction in the eyes of the Christian. His thoughts are not of the present possessors of the trim houses, the groves and gardens and vineyards outspread before him. His mind will wander far away among the dim shadows of the hoary past, calling up the shapes of the mighty who dwelt here of old. More than three thousand seven hundred years have passed away, since on that mountain top Abraham, "the friend of God," pleaded face to face with his Creator, in earnest intercession for sinning men. "The prayer of a righteous man availeth much," and great things were here granted by God to his faithful servant's prayer; but that long-suffering mercy brought no remission of punishment to the land that was so deeply flooded by the torrents of pollution.

And there David, the champion of his God and of his king, the fugitive outlaw, the sweet singer of Israel, the king over all the tribes of God's people, the inspired prophet, the deeply repentant sinner, the ancestor of the Messiah—stood by the city where first he reigned.

Here at length the traveller is now supposed to be within the border of civilization, and amongst a fixed population, dwelling in houses instead of amongst the nomade dwellers in tents. From henceforth, horses and mules are destined to carry him and his baggage; and the "ships of the desert" return to their native wilderness.

It is a matter of great interest to the traveller, with his Bible and his map before him, to study the relative positions of the town, the hills, and the ramifications of the valleys which intersect them, with the view of forming some definite opinion concerning Kirjath Arba (which is Hebron), Eshcol, and Mamre. Hebron is the position where he may best arrange his ideas, digest the information acquired, retrace his route through the hill country and its fenced cities, recall the associations their names have aroused, and weigh the arguments for and against the authenticity of the reputed sites of those cities which Judah won from the Canaanite.

Many of the places in sight of or near which one passes bear names often met with in Scripture; and whilst pausing at Hebron, a retrospective glance may be given to some of those in "the south country" that are most famous.

Sinai and Kadesh-Barnea stood out prominently in the story of the forty years' wandering; Hebron and Beersheba bear just the same relation to the ancient annals of the land of the Lion of Judah.

About six hours' journey to the westward of the ruins of the wells at Moladah, already mentioned, are other wells and other ruins of a place far more renowned in early Bible history, for they mark the undoubted site of *Beersheba*. Abraham dug the first "well of water" here; and here, too, he planted a grove, and in the shade of that natural temple offered up sacrifices, "and called there on the name of the Lord, the everlasting God." Here Abraham made a covenant with Abimelech, the Philistine sheikh of Gerar, to show friendship to his descendants to the third generation. Having sworn to this alliance, "Abraham reproved Abimelech because of a well of water which Abimelech's servants had violently taken away;" and then, no doubt in the presence of many spectators who could testify to the fact, gave him seven ewe lambs as "a witness" that he had digged the well, and that it was his for ever. Then it was that, in memorial of his covenant and oath, the patriarch gave the well the name of Beersheba, which is translated by some, "the well of the oath," and by others, "the well of the seven." That name it bears at the present time, for the Arabic "Bir es Seba" has the latter of the two significations of its Hebrew predecessor.

On this spot God talked with Abraham, and tried him, commanding him to sacrifice his son, his only son Isaac. From hence, without a moment's hesitation, but with more than child-like trust in, and ready obedience to, the commands of his Father in heaven, Abraham started early in the morning to offer up his son on the mountain in Moriah's land. He never faltered in that purpose nor doubted the Almighty, and won the blessing, "In thy seed shall all the nations of the earth be blessed;" and then he returned to Beersheba, and in Beersheba he dwelt.

At Beersheba, Isaac also pitched his tent when the Philistines, in jealousy

ABRAHAM'S OAK.

at his prosperity, drove him from place to place, the herdsmen of Abimelech (successor to him who had joined in the oath with Abraham) disputing with his servants about the wells they digged. Then Abraham's son renewed his father's covenant with Abimelech's successor, and digged another well in Beersheba. Here to him in his trouble, as to his father Abraham of yore, God appeared at night, and spoke the words of blessing and encouragement, "Fear not; for I am with thee, and will bless thee." Isaac built an altar, and called upon the name of the Lord; and, in like manner, all those who in their hearts erect an altar to the Lord, and, through his Son Jesus, in faith call on his name, need have no fears; for the God of Abraham, of Isaac, and of Jacob will watch over them.

At Beersheba it was that Jacob by subtilty took away his brother's blessing—deceit which cost him long years of exile from his mother's love and his father's face. When an old man himself, he came south to Hebron, and there he saw his father die; and afterwards, when he was on his road to Joseph in Egypt, he came again to Beersheba, and here he sacrificed to God.

In Beersheba, Samuel made his sons judges over Israel; and their wicked lives, coupled with Samuel's old age and the prospect that speedily the people would be left without a guide in whom they could trust, incited the Israelites, so prone to forget God's watchful care over them, to ask for a king.

Elijah, flying from Jezebel, "went for his life and came to Beersheba, which belongeth to Judah;" and going a day's journey further into the wilderness, rested and slept under one of the tall thick tufts of retem, or desert broom, and woke to partake of food supplied by miracle.

Beersheba was the southern limit of Palestine proper, which extended "from Dan to Beersheba." The only later mention of Beersheba in Scripture is the bare fact that the Jews returned thither after the captivity. In later times it was a small town with a Roman garrison. Afterwards it was the seat of a bishop, but it sank to a village, and finally was deserted. In the fourteenth century, Mandeville and other travellers relate that some of its churches were still standing.

Abraham's grove has disappeared with Judah's forests, and only a few stones and foundations scattered over the bare hill and valley mark the town's site; but the old wells still remain. The larger one measures twelve feet and a half in diameter, and is forty-four feet and a half to the water's brink. The smaller well is about the same depth, but is only five feet in diameter. Both of them still afford a copious supply of pure fresh spring water, and on this hallowed spot the wayfarer may drink from the well that Abraham dug, and ask a blessing from the God in whom Abraham trusted.

The far-famed tree called "The Oak of Abraham," is an object of interest. The patriarch sat in his tent door in the plains of Mamre, in the heat of the day; "and he lift up his eyes, and looked, and, lo, three men stood by him." As befitted the sheikh of a great pastoral tribe, and as many an Arab of meaner degree and poorer circumstances would do now, he went forward to meet the strangers, and pressed his hospitality upon them. They accepted it, and resting under the tree close to whose shade their host's tent was pitched, they partook of the fare he provided. The Lord, in human guise, was among these guests; and he then, under that tree in Mamre, renewed the promise that a son should be born to aged Abraham and to aged Sarah, who should inherit the blessings of the covenant. Tradition indicated a tree near Hebron as that under which the Lord and his angels had been the guests of man. There has been much controversy both as to the species of that tree and as to its actual position, it being almost impossible to reconcile the accounts given by various early writers, chief among whom are Josephus, Jerome, and Eusebius. They speak of the tree dignified by this tradition as a terebinth, and, whether oak or terebinth, it is difficult to form an accurate opinion as to its exact situation. In the time of our Saviour, a terebinth of immense size, and said to be as old as Adam, was venerated by the Jews as that which shaded the tent of their progenitor.

Whether or not the tree which existed in our Saviour's time was the original tree, we have no means of knowing. There seems to be no doubt that that tree was a terebinth, and it is probable that the real tree may have been an oak. There are now no large terebinths near Hebron.

In whatever epoch the terebinth of Jerome disappeared, the popular mind, no doubt, fixed upon the nearest tree of great age and size, and attached to it the tale and the honour. Succeeding generations received this successor, without question or doubt, as the original. The present "Oak of Abraham" is certainly not the tree mentioned in Genesis, though probably for many centuries it has borne that distinction. It is a kingly tree; the grandest and most picturesque in Palestine, south of Lebanon. It may be a thousand years old, possibly much more ancient; and it impresses one all the more from the marked absence of fine timber throughout this land. It is a prickly oak, called by the Arabs "Sindiân." The trunk is said to be 25 or 26 feet in girth. It rises from a great mass of gnarled and rugged roots, and almost immediately divides into three huge limbs. The branches extend from the trunk in one direction about 50 feet, and the whole diameter of their spread in this direction is 90 feet, and in another direction at right angles nearly 85 feet. A large limb torn off by some storm still lies near, dead upon the ground.

## VI.

## THE VALLEY OF ESHCOL.—FENCED CITIES OF JUDAH.

THE valley above Hebron is considered by most authorities to be the valley of Eshcol, whence the spies cut "one cluster of grapes, and bare it between two upon a staff, and brought of the pomegranates and of the figs," and carried them to all Israel at Kadesh, as evidence of the exuberant fruitfulness of the land that "surely flowed with milk and honey."

The locality is really in a mountain land. It constantly rises from the Arabah; and Hebron itself is the town of highest elevation in all Syria, standing two thousand eight hundred feet above the sea; so that truly Jacob and his sons "went down into Egypt." This considerable elevation, and its variable climate, caused the fertility which prompted Caleb to ask for the region round Hebron as his portion of the promised land, and which made that district so rich a reward. It is the mists, the moisture, and the cooler air of a more northern clime, conjoined with the fervid heat of the sun of a Syrian summer, that have made Eshcol's valley so celebrated. These same causes still work out similar results, and the vines of Eshcol's vale still bear splendid grapes, the largest and best in all the country round; figs and pomegranates burden the trees on the terraced mountain sides, whose groves likewise enrich her with "oil olive," and the fields wave with corn.

This is the first place seen in all the border-land of the south, in which one can appreciate the longing of Abraham's children for the land God had promised them. Here, indeed, is a fair example of that country which was "a land of corn and wine, a land of bread and vineyards, a land of oil olive and honey," and of which we read so much.

The vines in the vicinity of Hebron are sometimes enclosed in vineyards surrounded by stone walls, and overlooked by "the tower of the watchman;" sometimes they run along terraces which may have existed from the early days of Israel's possession, and here and there is built a hut for the guards or vine-dressers —"a cottage in a vineyard." In these towers and huts, and also in tents, the families of Hebron are crowded in time of vintage, which is a festival season for the whole population; and the town is left deserted. The produce of the vineyards is sent all over Palestine. The proprietors, being chiefly Mohammedans make no wine or raki; but a little is made by the Jews, though not in sufficient quantities for exportation. The best grapes are made into raisins; the remainder are trodden out in the winepress, and their juice is boiled down to a syrup, which resembles treacle, but has a pleasanter taste. This syrup is called "dibs," a Hebrew word signifying "honey" and also "syrup of grapes;" and wherever in Palestine there is "a land of vineyards" this syrup is commonly eaten with bread.

Before proceeding northward some notice is requisite of the south country, and of the fenced cities of Judah, near which the road to Hebron passes. Something more about Hebron itself will be said before proceeding onwards. Beersheba and Moladah have been already mentioned: it is after leaving the latter place—the modern El Milh—that ruins and hills, many of them still bearing their old historic names exactly, and others preserving with some slight modification the nomenclature of Joshua's days, begin to crowd upon the traveller.

Attir, Anâb, Main, Kurmel, Yutta, Zif, Shuweikeh, names now in use for existing localities, speak to us of Yattir, Anab, Maon, Carmel, Juttah, Ziph, and Socoh, so called when Judah first took possession of his heritage. Maon, Carmel, and Ziph are a little to the right, with the wilderness of Engedi beyond them. These names are especially familiar, for it was in this district that Saul hunted David like "a partridge in the mountains." This "wilderness of Maon" and this "wilderness of Ziph" harboured David "in the rocks of the wild goats," in caves and forests, which were then the haunt of lions and other wild beasts. Both the lions and the forests have long since disappeared; but the grey hills, the deep caves, the scattered ruins, and the old names still remain.

Many an eventful story are we told of David's adventures here; but in all the records of his wild career there is no tale more strangely romantic than that of which Maon and Carmel were the scene.

In Maon, on the top of that high, bare, conical hill, now crowned with ruins, dwelt the "churlish and evil" Nabal, "whose possessions were in Carmel." He was a worthless offshoot of the house of the mighty Caleb; but no portion of Caleb's virtues had descended to Nabal with Caleb's land. He was rich in flocks, and he was, at the date of the narrative, shearing his sheep in Carmel. At that time, David and his armed men, outlaws and fugitives like himself, were hiding in the neighbouring wilderness; and day by day Nabal's pastoral wealth, and those who tended it, had been at the mercy of David's band, without suffering diminution or hurt; but, on the contrary, they had been "a wall unto them both by night and by day." David consequently expected to share in the feast prepared for the shearers, as any modern Arab sheikh of the wilderness, who had protected the flocks of his rich neighbour, would on a similar occasion. He sent

THE VALLEY OF ESHCOL.

messengers to greet Nabal, in the words that any native of Palestine would use at the present time:—"Thus shall ye say to him that liveth in prosperity, Peace be both to thee, and peace be to thine house, and peace be unto all that thou hast." Then he set forth his claim for a portion of the food that was in preparation; but his request was met by Nabal with contumely and railing. "Who is David? and who is the son of Jesse? There be many servants now-a-days that break away every man from his master. Shall I then take my bread and my water, and my flesh that I have killed for my shearers, and give it unto men whom I know not whence they be?"

Nabal had a wife, named Abigail, "and she was a woman of a good understanding and of a beautiful countenance;" and she and Nabal's servants knew his character well, "that he was such a son of Belial that a man cannot speak to him." They also seem to have rightly estimated the probable vigour of David's rejoinder, for Abigail sent to David provisions which were luxuries compared with those which he would have been satisfied with, and which her lord had refused; and then she set forth herself to meet him. She was only just in time, for the sword was girded on the thigh, and David was already on his way to the slaughter of Nabal and his race. But God designed otherwise, and made use of woman's gentle tact, and woman's persuasive tongue, as his instruments to check his servant in the career of blood, and to save him from sin.

Abigail, in her mediation, did not attempt to deny her husband's wrongdoing, or to gloss over his churlishness; but with the fear of God in her heart, she argued gently and firmly with David's hot wrath. She knew that God designed him to rule over Israel. She advised the future monarch neither to shed blood nor to avenge himself with his own hand; and then, speaking of that future time when he should reign over all the tribes of God's people, she said: "This shall be no grief unto thee, nor offence of heart unto my lord, either that thou hast shed blood causeless, or that my lord hath avenged himself; but when the Lord shall have dealt well with my lord, then remember thine handmaid." David's anger was checked, and he gave glory to the Almighty, and gratitude to Abigail, as God's instrument, for her wise counsel, which had saved him from crime; and how earnest and heartfelt is the expression of that gratitude! "Blessed be the Lord God of Israel, which sent thee this day to meet me; and blessed be thy advice; and blessed be thou which hast kept me this day from coming to shed blood, and from avenging myself with mine own hand."

David and Abigail parted and went their ways; he to his hiding-place in the wilderness, she to where her husband, in fancied security, "held a feast in his house like the feast of a king," where, but for her intercession, blood would have flowed as freely as did the wine with which "Nabal's heart was merry within him, for he was very drunken." In the morning his good wife told him the danger he had incurred, and the mode of his escape. Then his boldness all fled, and "his heart died within him, and he became as a stone." About ten days after, God smote Nabal that he died, and left those riches whose stewardship he had so flagrantly abused. David's first thought at the news of Nabal's death was one of thankfulness to the Lord who had kept his servant from evil. His second was for Abigail's wisdom and beauty. He at once sent messengers to her, and she became his wife.

It should be here mentioned, to prevent confusion of ideas, that this "Carmel," where Nabal had his possessions, is far distant from Mount Carmel, to the north, on the Phœnician coast, the scene of Elijah's sacrifice. The ruins of this southern Carmel in Judah are extensive, and some of them very ancient. The castle, from the style of its masonry, is probably of the time of Herod. Among the ruins are the remains of churches, showing that Carmel had at one time a large Christian population. It is all desert now. About an hour and a half from Carmel is the little hill "Tell Zif," close to which are the ruins of Ziph, whose people on two occasions betrayed David's hiding-place to Saul. On the first occasion David was "in a mountain in the wilderness of Ziph," and though "Saul sought him every day," yet "God delivered him not into his hand;" and here it was that Jonathan gave another proof of his strong, tender, and life-long affection for the son of Jesse, for he "went to David into the wood and strengthened his hand in God."

In all history, sacred and profane, there is no more touching example of true, unselfish, unwavering devotion of man to man than that of Jonathan for David. Jonathan knew that his friend would deprive him of the throne to which he might, but for him, succeed; but no thought of self entered his mind. He knew that it was the will of Jehovah that David should rule Israel, and he bowed his heart without a murmur to that almighty will, and rejoiced in the thought that his friend would be his king. David now wandered into the wilderness of Maon for a time, and after that the Ziphites again betrayed his haunts to Saul, who sought him in the wilderness of Ziph with three thousand chosen men of Israel. To no purpose; for the Lord watched over David, who penetrated Saul's camp at night, and took the spear and cruse of water from beside the bolster of the sleeping king. God here specially interposed in David's behalf; for "no man saw it nor knew it, neither awaked; for they were all asleep, because a deep sleep from the Lord was fallen upon them." David spared his enemy when in his power, and God preserved him from all danger.

## VII.

## ANTIQUITY OF HEBRON.—THE POOLS OF SOLOMON.

The world after the flood must have been young when Hebron was founded. Scripture tells us that it was built "seven years before Zoan in Egypt;" but who can tell when that was, for Zoan has disappeared, leaving no trace? All that we know for certain is, that it was a walled city when Abraham's tent was pitched in Mamre; for when Sarah died, and he sought a tomb for her, "the field of Ephron which was in Machpelah which was before Mamre, the field and the cave that was therein, and all the trees that were in the field, that were in all the borders round about, were made sure unto Abraham for a possession in the presence of the children of Heth before all that went in at the gate of his city:" "the same is Hebron, in the land of Canaan." From that early date almost continuously down to the present day, it has been an inhabited city. It has always been of considerable importance, though probably it has never been very extensive. The earliest associations that cling round its name are all connected with Abraham.

If a great nomad chief, such as Abraham was, can be said to have had any home, Abraham's home was at Hebron. Here took place many of the most awe-inspiring events of his wonderful career, for here he talked with God as with a friend, and here he was permitted to argue with the Almighty. Hebron in its present name preserves a remembrance of Abraham's intimate communion with God.

It has borne several names, and probably its most ancient appellation is unknown to us; but at any rate at an early period it was called Kirjath Arba, the city of Arba—"which Arba was a great man among the Anakims." For a time it seems to have been called "Mamre," and to have belonged to Abraham's friend and ally in his expedition to rescue Lot and his family from the four kings. Then, when Caleb captured it from the descendants of Anak and Arba, it received from him the name most familiar to us, "Hebron," which, however, has been forgotten for ages in this land. In the time of the Crusades, the citadel to the north of the great edifice over the tombs of the patriarchs was called "the Castle of Abraham," and this name was used as including the town as well. By the Moslems, Abraham is called "El Khulil," "The Friend" (of God), and they gave this name to the city around his sepulchre, and by this name is it now known.

Hebron is an unquestioned site. No one has hazarded a doubt upon the subject; so that we may feel confident that it stands in close proximity to the old city, and probably occupies part of its area, as the houses of the modern town skirt the pools that belonged to David's capital.

Two reservoirs of great antiquity still supply Hebron with water. The lower pool is 133 feet square, built with hewn stone, and is 22 feet deep. The upper pool is 85 feet by 55 feet, and 19 feet deep. There is every probability that one of these two great tanks was "the pool in Hebron," over which David hanged up the hands and feet of Rechab and Baanah, the murderers of Ishbosheth, Saul's son. Jewish traditions attribute the construction of these pools to Solomon, ignorantly confounding them with the famous pools on the road between Hebron and Jerusalem. To Hebron, after Ishbosheth's death, the tribes of Israel came, and here they anointed David as their king.

When Judah was led into captivity, Hebron was destroyed, and it was during this period, if ever, that it remained for a time uninhabited; but upon the return of the Jews from Babylon it was rebuilt. It then fell into the hands of the Edomites, from whom Judas Maccabeus recaptured it. In A.D. 1167 it was made a Latin bishopric by the Crusaders; but from A.D. 1187 till the present time it has been possessed altogether by the Moslems, who erected there a great mosque, which is one of the most remarkable structures in Palestine.

That the cave of Machpelah is inclosed within the walls of the great mosque there is good reason to believe from the warranty of unbroken tradition, extending from patriarchal times to our own epoch.

A ride of about three hours from the Oak of Abraham reaches the far-famed Pools of Solomon. A characteristic fragment of which, including part of the two upper pools and the extensive Saracenic fort, intended most probably to guard the approach to Jerusalem, is given in the picture.

The pools are vast reservoirs constructed in a descending valley, so that the bottom of the upper pool is higher than the margin of the one next below it. The upper pool is the smallest, and the lower one the largest. The first measures 380 feet long; it is 25 feet deep, and 236 feet wide at the eastern end. The western extremity is seven feet narrower. The middle pool is 423 feet long, 39 feet deep, and of the same width as the upper pool, 236 feet. It is 160 feet below the upper pool. The lower pool is 248 feet further down the valley than the middle pool; it is 582 feet long, 50 feet deep; but it is only 207 feet wide at its eastern extremity, and 148 feet wide at its western end. Of these pools, and of the glory of their maker, Solomon, we shall speak further.

THE POOLS OF SOLOMON.

## VIII.

## SOLOMON'S WORKS—THE TOWER OF DAVID.

Solomon's peaceful reign gave him ample leisure for applying his mind to study and reflection. In theory, his "heart had great experience of wisdom and knowledge;" but he determined to win practical experience for himself, and to test the pleasures, the luxuries, the joys, the interests, the labours of rich and poor—the aims, the struggles of life—with a view to estimate properly their value and their power in themselves to make man happy and contented during the progress of his earthly pilgrimage. He tried fully, and tasted often of mirth and laughter, of wisdom, of pleasure, and folly, even of knowledge carefully acquired, and of labour guided by a successful issue; but ere from the cup of enjoyment the draught of satisfied desire was fully drained, there ever rose to his lips some bitter drop. God's grace at length guided Solomon's heart to a right conclusion, and the injunction he gives to all posterity is, "Fear God." Solomon found that for those who feared God and placed themselves in his hands, there was no bitter drop lingering in the cup that held their draught of life.

It was while he was thus testing the good the earth contained, only to find that without God it was nought, that he tells us, "I made me great works; I builded me houses; I planted me vineyards; I made me gardens and orchards, and I planted trees in them of all kinds of fruits; I made me pools of water to water therewith the wood that bringeth forth trees;" and right royally did the sumptuous monarch work out his experiment. "My wisdom remained with me, and whatsoever mine eyes desired I kept not from them; I withheld not my heart from any joy, for my heart rejoiced in all my labour."

The delicious gardens to which king Solomon was wont in his majesty to ride prosperously, were made at Etham, about fifty stadia from Jerusalem.

Nearly a mile below the pools described before, the ruined village of Urtas stands in a narrow rocky glen. This is the site of Etham; here was that "garden enclosed," fragrant with spices, radiant with flowers, and bountiful in fruits. Down to its terraces, from the "pools of water" Solomon made, and from "a spring shut up, a fountain sealed," streamlets flowed to water and fertilize the garden.

At Urtas still exist the foundations of a strong tower, a ruined wall of hewn stone, and grottoes and excavations in the rocks, to which have been added small outworks of hovels or sheds by the present inhabitants of Solomon's retreat; and in this mixed kind of dwelling they live, more than half underground.

In the bed of the glen, whose sides now are stony and barren, there is a small oasis of luxuriant garden, watered by a spring that rises near. One of Solomon's kindred by blood—an Israelite who believes in Christ crucified—tills the fruitful soil and gathers an abundant return for his labour.

Once a fortnight, one of the English missionaries in Jerusalem comes hither to perform service with this convert from Judaism and his family.

The "pools of water" which Solomon made are partly excavated in the rock and partly built of great hewn stones. From the source which supplies them, an aqueduct winds through hill and dale to Jerusalem, and ends in the Haram, where of old the temple stood. The distance is long, its winding course being from twelve to fourteen miles. Water still flows through a considerable portion of the aqueduct.

The copious spring which, according to the Talmud, supplied the Temple and also watered the gardens of its builder, is in the open field above the pools. All that is visible above-ground at the source is a round hole like the mouth of a well, covered with a huge stone. Descending through this opening for twelve feet, a vault, roofed with ancient and handsome stone arches, is reached. This chamber is about 45 feet long and 24 feet broad; and another similar vault, somewhat smaller, adjoins it. The water rises in four places, and is conveyed first into a basin and then by a large subterraneous passage towards the pools, into which part of it falls, the rest being diverted by the aqueduct. To keep up a constant supply for the Temple, there was a branch channel from the second pool to the aqueduct. Another aqueduct, also, formerly conducted the waters of a spring, situated among the hills more to the south, into the lower pool.

The picturesque building at the upper pool is called Kalat el Burak, and was intended as a fort and a caravansera combined; dating from the Crusades.

The entrance to Jerusalem by the "Jaffa Gate," or "Hebron Gate," is in the citadel, the stronghold of modern Jerusalem in the days of the Crusades. An engraving is given of its most prominent feature, the "Tower of David," or the "Tower of Hippicus" as it almost indubitably is: it is one of the most important relics of the many splendid edifices Herod raised.

THE TOWER OF DAVID, JERUSALEM.

## IX.

## ROUTE FROM HEBRON TO JERUSALEM.—THE POOL OF HEZEKIAH.

Leaving Hebron, on the way to Jerusalem, for some distance the road lies between the high walls which inclose the vineyards: in some places it is paved with loose blocks of stone, and is very rough and uneven; in other parts it passes over solid rock, worn into holes by constant traffic; but in spite of these asperities, it is not a bad road over which to ride a sure-footed Syrian Arab. Emerging from the valleys of Mamre and Eshcol, the vines and olive trees, the well-built terraces, and the abundant springs are left behind, and the course lies over wild hills, some being quite bare, while others are covered with brushwood, dwarf oak, and arbutus. The soil in the valleys is rich, and the hill sides are all seamed with the marks of ancient terraces, indicating the careful cultivation carried on here of old. Now they only afford scanty pasturage for flocks. Many ruins, varying in character and extent, are passed, especially near Hebron. The village of Halhûl stands on the site of the Hulhul mentioned in Joshua, and soon after the remains of a large building with a fountain near it are seen. The rocks around are scarped perpendicularly and excavated, probably for tombs, which may have been constructed by the Edomites during their possession of the district. This is the site of Bethzur, and a half ruined tower is called by the Arabs Beit Sûr.

As in the south country, the hills are sometimes crowned with grey ruins of ancient towns, and sometimes with massive towers of defence or border forts. The number of ruins passed after entering Palestine is extraordinary, and testifies both to the fertility of the land under its pristine conditions, and to the numerous inhabitants who dwelt throughout its whole extent. With the sole exception of Hebron, destruction has fallen upon all the edifices raised by man, from " the tower of the watchman to the fenced city."

Approaching Solomon's Pools, there is at one point a magnificent view to the westward towards Philistia, through a cleft in the hills. This road, from Hebron to Jerusalem, was for the whole of the last century quite unfrequented by pilgrims or Frank travellers: during that period no one appears to have visited Hebron; and for many years previously its visitors had been but few. In the fourteenth century it was on the high road of the pilgrims between Sinai and Jerusalem, and many went hither from the holy city who did not adventure upon the risks and hardships of the desert pilgrimage to Sinai. In those times there was a hospital or institution at Hebron, where charity was dispensed on a vast scale. Twelve hundred loaves of bread, besides oil and other articles of food, were distributed daily to all comers, of all creeds and nationalities. The annual expenses were estimated at twenty-four thousand ducats, part of which was derived from property in the neighbourhood belonging to the hospital. In the fifteenth century, pilgrims began to take the Gaza route; and in the next century that by Hebron was almost deserted. From that time till the year 1806, Hebron was quite lost sight of; but then Seetzen succeeded in reaching it, on his road from Sinai, and Ali Bey followed him the next year. Eleven years later it was visited by Captains Irby and Mangles; and thirteen years afterwards by Poujoulat. Monro also, in 1833, reached it from Jerusalem. Since 1835 there have been no difficulties sufficient to deter travellers from including the city of the patriarchs amongst the sacred sites they may visit in Palestine.

Shortly after passing Solomon's Pools, the aspect of the country begins to improve; and, looking back, the traveller gets glimpses of Bethlehem and of a pretty village called Beit Jâla, beautifully situated on a hill slope, embowered amidst olive and fruit-tree groves. Here the Latin patriarch of Jerusalem has a palace, and a large church has also been built by the Roman Catholics.

Close to the road is a building claiming remark, for there was buried Rachel, the lovely and the loved. Passing on and ascending a hill, the convent of Mar Elias is reached.

Jerusalem now comes in sight, bereft, on this approach, of all the characteristics of her imposing position. A road, or rather a track across a plain, leads straight up to a line of grey, unpicturesque buildings at a distance; so that the walls and domes of the city seem to be built in the middle of the arable land. There is no indication of the deep ravine which separates from the lofty and precipitous brow on which the Temple stood; for the level table-land only terminates upon the brink of the southern declivity, bounding the valley of Hinnom.

The plain or valley on the left was that of Rephaim, "the Valley of the Giants." Along the road here traversed, David, the newly-anointed king of Israel, marched to take possession of his future capital. Its then possessors

THE POOL OF HEZEKIAH.

defied the Lord's anointed; "nevertheless David took the stronghold of Zion; the same is the city of David;" and then "David dwelt in the fort, and called it the city of David." Then the Philistines heard of his accession, and marched against him, "and spread themselves in the valley of Rephaim;" and "David inquired of the Lord, saying, Shall I go up to the Philistines, and wilt thou deliver them into my hand? And the Lord said unto David, Go up, for I will doubtless deliver the Philistines into thine hand." David obeyed; he smote the Philistines, who left their images behind in their flight, "and David and his men burned them." Again the Philistines "spread themselves in the valley of Rephaim;" and this time again David inquired of the Lord, who commanded him not to meet them, but to "fetch a compass behind them," and when he heard "the sound of a going in the tops of the mulberry trees," he was to bestir himself, for the Lord was then going before him to the slaughter of the Philistine host. Again David obeyed, and the Lord performed his word given to his servant. The plain of Rephaim was probably well known for its fertility, for Isaiah alludes to him that "gathereth ears in the valley of Rephaim."

Crossing the valley of Hinnom, the traveller mounts the steep path to the citadel. Many are the theories concerning the hills, the walls, the gates, the extent of the city, and about the positions of the great buildings they enclosed; but although a great diversity of opinion exists respecting the ancient boundaries of Jerusalem, yet that mount on which stands the citadel—the tower or castle of David—is certainly Mount Zion, the stronghold David won from the Jebusites.

Upon Mount Zion in later days stood Herod's palace; and in the city wall, on the crest of Mount Zion, he built three splendid towers, called by the names of his valiant and ill-fated friend, his devoted and unfortunate brother, and his loved but murdered wife—Hippicus, Phasaëlus, and Mariamne. These towers were a marvel of workmanship, beauty, and strength. There is little doubt that among the strong towers and massive walls of the citadel of Jerusalem—the castle of David—there exists a relic of Herod's fortifications; for one ancient tower has been identified as that of Hippicus, which we are told was built up entirely solid to the height of thirty cubits. It is the prevailing opinion that the particular tower in the citadel commonly called "the tower of David" is in reality that of Hippicus.

When Titus destroyed Jerusalem, he left standing Herod's three towers, with part of the western wall of Zion, both as a citadel for the soldiers he placed in garrison at Jerusalem, and as a monument to future ages of the vast strength of the fenced city Roman valour had overthrown.

E

The modern citadel is composed of an irregular group of square towers, protected on the outer side by a deep fosse, with a sloping bulwark of ancient masonry, which seems of Roman workmanship, and was most likely constructed by Adrian, when he rebuilt the city. On the inner side, a low wall runs round the towers. The north-eastern tower, for about forty feet of its height, is built of huge bevelled blocks, from nine to thirteen feet long, and four feet high; above this it is of modern construction. Its dimensions are a little more than seventy feet by fifty-six feet. There is no entrance, either on one side or from above, to the ancient portion of the tower, and no one knew of any chamber in it. This evidence, so far as it goes, of a want of vacuity, in the mass of this ancient structure, has been corroborated by the discovery that the lower part is of solid rock, cut into shape, and faced with masonry, tallying so completely in this respect with the account given by Josephus, as almost to establish for certain its identity with the tower of Hippicus.

This tower is a definite point of the greatest value in attempts to trace the walls and discover the chief localities of the city which saw the completion of the Redeemer's mission upon earth, for Josephus makes it the starting-point in his description of the course of the first and third walls of the city; and unless we can establish the position of Hippicus, the account of Josephus will be unintelligible, and consequently useless.

There is much ancient masonry in the lower part of the walls and towers of the citadel, partly, no doubt, the remains of Adrian's fortress. When the Crusaders took Jerusalem in A.D. 1099, this citadel was the stronghold of the city, and the last point surrendered to them. In those days it was called the "tower" or "castle" of David, and is described as being very strong, and built of large hewn stones. It derived its name either from its proximity to David's tomb, or from the belief that it was built by that monarch. When the Moslems destroyed the walls of the city, in A.D. 1219, they spared the citadel, and the Franks continued to give it the name of "the tower of David" till the sixteenth century, when it was called "the castle of the Pisans," in consequence of a belief that it had been repaired by citizens of that republic.

Near the citadel is a picturesque and ancient pool or tank, which forms the subject of the illustration. It is commonly called "the Pool of Hezekiah." A Coptic convent stands on its brink, and over the roofs appear the tower and dome of the church of the Holy Sepulchre.

## X.

### JERUSALEM—THE TOMBS OF DAVID AND HIS SUCCESSORS—THE "LARGE UPPER ROOM"—VIA DOLOROSA—ARCH OF ECCE HOMO.

On the first view of Jerusalem, the aspect that the city presents to the majority of travellers approaching her walls—those coming by all the most frequented routes, from Joppa, from Gaza, from Hebron, and also to a certain extent from Damascus—is anything but striking or impressive. Many travellers, who have visited in a true pilgrim spirit the land where our Saviour's earthly pilgrimage was performed, have expressed their great disappointment on first seeing the holy city. But though at the first sight of Jerusalem we may not be affected altogether according to our expectations, yet none the less will Jerusalem and all that belongs to it make a deep and lasting impression upon the mind, when calmly and quietly, from the slope of Olivet, or the brow of the Mount of Offence, or the summit of the Hill of Evil Counsel, we gaze on the scene of those sufferings and that death which consummated the Divine work of redemption.

The English church at Jerusalem is well built and sufficiently handsome. It is attached to the English consulate, and thus obtains the advantage of British protection in a greater degree than it would if it were altogether isolated. In excavating for its foundations, some interesting discoveries were made. In digging downwards to find some secure resting-place for the foundation stones, conclusive proof was afforded of the entire subversion of all the palaces, private houses, and public buildings, which successively stood upon Mount Zion. It was necessary to descend for nearly forty feet before a sound foundation could be reached. All above that depth was ruins. The first stone was laid upon the solid rock of Mount Zion, on the 28th of January, 1842, at a depth of thirty-five feet below the surface, which was not the greatest depth attained by the foundations. In excavating the last shaft for one of the foundation piers, an immense conduit was discovered, partly hewn out of the rock, partly built of solid masonry, and lined with cement an inch thick. It is probable that this is the conduit of Hezekiah, by which he brought the waters of the fountain of Gihon to the west side of the city of David.

A large proportion of the plateau of Mount Zion lies without the present walls of the city; and in advance of these walls, on the brow of the hill to the southward, stands a group of buildings, one of which is supposed to cover the rock-hewn tombs of king David and his successors. That David, when he slept with his fathers, was buried in the city of David, is certain. The word of God tells us plainly that such was the fact, and also that fourteen succeeding monarchs who sat on the throne of Jerusalem were buried on Mount Zion, but not all of them with their father David in the sepulchre of the kings. It is probable that the sepulchres of the kings were grouped together in an open space, or "field," the tombs being excavated in the rock, the monuments above them standing on Zion's brow. Nehemiah incidentally describes the situation of these tombs in his account of the rebuilding of the walls of Jerusalem, and his description leads us to suppose that the sepulchres must be upon the southern brow of Zion, either at or close to their reported site. Josephus says that Solomon buried David with great pomp, and placed immense treasures along with his body in the tomb.

The situation of these tombs was well known in apostolic times; for St. Peter, speaking of David, says, "He is both dead and buried, and his sepulchre is with us unto this day." In the fifteenth century, the tombs are referred to by several travellers, one of whom, Tucher of Nuremberg, A.D. 1479, says that the Moslems had converted the crypt or lower story of the Cœnaculum into a mosque, within which were shown the tombs of David, Solomon, and the other kings. For upwards of four centuries, Christians, Jews, and Moslems have agreed in regarding the mosque on Zion as the spot beneath which lie the royal sepulchres of Judah's kings, and Jews may often be seen gazing sadly upon the ancient building within whose walls they may not enter, and which probably for near fifteen centuries has covered the royal psalmist's dust.

In this edifice is a large upper chamber, about fifty feet long by thirty wide, that had been apparently a church of great antiquity. This chamber claims by tradition descending from an early period, to be the "large upper room" where our Saviour celebrated the passover with his disciples. In this room, too, it is said that the disciples were assembled at Pentecost, when they were all filled with the Holy Ghost. Other legends soon grouped themselves around this spot. Arculf (A.D. 700) found that within the area covered by this building, the Virgin Mary died and St. Stephen was martyred; and yet later

THE VIA DOLOROSA.

the monks added other occurrences of interest to the long list of events connected with our Saviour's earthly career, supposed to have taken place here.

The most comfortable residence in Jerusalem is unquestionably the great Armenian convent, which with its buildings and gardens covers a large proportion of that part of the summit of Mount Zion which is inclosed within the city wall. It is a noble and vast institution, and can afford accommodation to three thousand pilgrims.

These are the sites upon Mount Zion most distinguished by their past associations, the remainder with a long list omitted have been the suggestions of knaves or enthusiasts.

A few words more upon time-honoured Zion before entering the later-built city,

This "stronghold of Zion," the hill fort of the Jebusites, was the parent of Jerusalem—the original nucleus of the city which Titus destroyed. Probably Salem, the royal city of Melchizedek, stood here, and no doubt it was the first spot occupied by buildings in the area of what was afterwards Jerusalem. It saw the last struggle between the Jew and the Roman, when the rest of Jerusalem was in ruins, and the soldiers of Titus filled the blood-stained courts of God's desecrated temple.

The mount of Zion was remarkably adapted by nature for a fenced city. The almost level platform on its summit gave ample space for habitations, and was bounded on three sides by craggy declivities falling into deep ravines. From the earliest times, the resources of art had added to the natural defences, and we have seen how its ancient possessors defied David and David's God. He took the hill fortress, enlarged, adorned, and strengthened it, till he made it worthy to be Israel's capital; and then in many a passage we read how dear to the warrior-king were those mighty ramparts whose protection he could, from his own personal experience, so keenly appreciate, and how enthusiastic was his admiration of its majesty and beauty.

For some centuries a narrow street, which zigzags through the modern Jerusalem from the church of the Holy Sepulchre to the palace of the governor, has been called the "Via Dolorosa." Into this street tradition has brought together the scenes of all the events, historical or legendary, connected with the crucifixion. The legendary sites begin at the palace of Pontius Pilate, now the governor's palace, with two old built-up arches in the wall which mark the threshold of the "Scala Santa"— the holy staircase — down which our Saviour descended from the judgment hall, and which was transported by Constantine to the basilica of St. John Lateran at Rome, where, on days of high festival, crowds may be seen wearily toiling up step by step on their knees. Next, the "Arch of the Ecce Homo" spans the street. This is the subject of the engraving. From the window in the centre of the arch, Pilate is said to have exhibited Jesus to the multitude with the exclamation, "Behold the man!" The woman and child represented in the foreground are from living specimens.

Continuing onwards, the spot is shown where the Saviour, fainting under the cross, leaned against the wall of a house, and is said to have left a deep impression upon the stone. Then, there is the spot where, meeting his mother, he said, "Salve Mater!" and likewise the reputed house of Dives, and the stone in front of it on which Lazarus sat. Then there is the place where our Saviour fell with the cross, and, close by, the house of St. Veronica, whose identical handkerchief, tripled by some Romish miracle not recorded, is exhibited at Rome and at two other Italian cities at one and the same time. The street now ascends towards the church of the Holy Sepulchre, and is very picturesque, and from this point is taken our sketch of the Via Dolorosa. The pavement is rugged, and the houses rather prison-like. Their entrance doors are low, and the windows grated or covered with cupboard-like projections, pierced with small holes or latticed, to enable their inhabitants to look up and down the street. These projecting windows, when they occur, break the monotony of the otherwise blank walls. The street often dives under low archways and is almost dark; and here are more "stations," among which is the spot where the soldiers compelled Simon to carry the cross, and the place where Christ said to the weeping women, "Daughters of Jerusalem, weep not for me."

Now it is childish to suppose that this narrow street, with its sharp turns and twists, precisely followed the course of one of the great thoroughfares of the ancient city, after its almost total destruction, and the lapse of many centuries; and even if such an absurdity could be credited, it would but little assist in the identification of the sites enumerated. Still, these houses and walls and arches and stones are implicitly believed by pilgrims to mark the actual spots where the scenes we have referred to really took place, and a small knot of strangers, devout and believing, may often be seen gazing reverently on the spots hallowed by such associations.

The two views of this "Via Dolorosa" give a good idea of the street architecture of modern Jerusalem, and no better specimens could be found than these, which occur at intervals throughout its windings. Its name is mentioned by none of the early writers; the first allusion to it being in Marinus Sanutus, who wrote in the fourteenth century. We may therefore presume that its name and its "stations" are inventions of ecclesiastics.

THE ARCH OF THE ECCE HOMO.

## XI.
## GETHSEMANE.

The even was come, and Christ sat down with his twelve chosen followers, in the large upper room near the grave of his forefather in the flesh, to that repast which Christian churches of all creeds have held in continual remembrance. The eventful meal was ended; "and when they had sung a hymn, they went out into the Mount of Olives." "And they came to a place which was named Gethsemane; and he saith to his disciples, Sit ye here, while I shall pray. And he taketh with him Peter and James and John, and began to be sore amazed, and to be very heavy; and saith unto them, My soul is exceeding sorrowful unto death: tarry ye here, and watch. And he went forward a little, and fell on the ground, and prayed that, if it were possible, the hour might pass from him."

It was night, and the wearied apostles slumbered, while the dire struggle that was to work out their salvation was inaugurated; and upon the frail humanity of even those favoured three, who were especially chosen to give their Master companionship in his dread hour of sorrow, Jesus could not rely for one hour of wakeful sympathy. There, beneath the grey olive boughs, silvered by the pure rays of the clear moon, He who had put on mortality strove against mortal terror at the approaching hour of death. There, alone among the olive trees, he prayed, "Father, if thou be willing, remove this cup from me; nevertheless, not my will, but thine be done." And then "there appeared unto him an angel from heaven, strengthening him; and being in an agony, he prayed more earnestly; and his sweat was as it were great drops of blood falling down to the ground."

Hither, through the shadowy olive groves, came Judas with a band of men and officers from the chief priests and Pharisees, and with one kiss betrayed at once his Master's life and his own soul. Here, among the grey old trees, Peter, the loving, the hasty, the zealous, the unstable, smote the high priest's servant with the sword, and gave the mighty spiritual Physician an opportunity of working for the last time on earth a miracle of healing upon a mortal's ailing frame. He, who could command the help of legions of angels—He, at whose simple word the great multitude, with their lanterns and torches and weapons, went backwards and fell to the ground—wanted not the aid of a man's feeble sword, but of his own will took the cup his Father gave him, and drank it to the dregs, that so the Scripture might be fulfilled. Here, amidst the shadows of the pale groves, with calm, resolute purpose, and unalterable determination of heart, he stood forth boldly as the Captain of our salvation, to be made "perfect through suffering."

Descending the Via Dolorosa, up which it is related that Christ bore his cross, going forth by St. Stephen's Gate, and down a steep hill into the depths of the Valley of Jehoshaphat, and crossing a bridge over the almost dry watercourse of the Brook Kidron, we come to a group of aged olive trees, surrounded by a high white wall. This enclosure is at the very foot of the Mount of Olives, and here or hereabouts was that garden over the Brook Kidron, whither Jesus was wont to go forth with his disciples. "And Judas also which betrayed him knew the place, for Jesus oft-times resorted thither with his disciples." That garden was Gethsemane.

More than fifteen centuries ago, tradition pointed out the space encompassed by the wall as the real spot where the dread scene of the "agony" took place; and, doubtless, the ancient trees which that wall hedges in stand within or upon the verge of the Garden of Gethsemane. Here, under just such aged olive trees as these, perhaps beneath trees that sprang from the self-same roots which now supply these with sap, the disciples may have slumbered. A little further on, Peter, James, and John, out-wearied with their sorrow, may have slept; whilst their Lord, seeking a more secluded spot, went onward along the base of the hill, and "was withdrawn from them about a stone's cast, and kneeled down and prayed."

Perhaps on this very spot all the events recounted occurred, or possibly the absolute site may have been one or two hundred yards further along the foot of Olivet. At any rate, we may feel confident, if we wander for two or three hundred yards through these scattered olives, that our feet have pressed the sacred soil of Gethsemane's garden.

The Latin ecclesiastics, not long ago, got exclusive possession of the plot of ground mentioned above, and built the wall round it. Not, however, for the sake of protecting the trees, but to enable them to levy toll upon all those strangers and pilgrims who would naturally visit the sacred garden. Though the space within the wall is only about eighty yards square, it yields a better revenue than many and many an acre of corn-land and olive-yard would render; and all toil of cultivation is saved. To stimulate the liberality of the ignorant and blindly credulous pilgrims, a number of holy places are exhibited by the monks within this narrow space. They show a rocky bank where the disciples

THE GARDEN OF GETHSEMANE, AS IT IS.

slept whilst their Lord prayed, and point out the impressions left by their bodies upon the hard stone. Then they take the pilgrim to the "Grotto of the Agony," a cave in which they say our Saviour's prayers were offered up; and then they point out the exact spot where Judas stood, where he betrayed his Master with a kiss. This Latin speculation has paid so well, that the Greeks have enclosed a similar space close by, and stand up for their plot of garden ground as the genuine Gethsemane. The Armenians are about to follow their example. The Greeks have not been so fortunate in the trees surrounded by the wall they have lately built, as their Latin brethren, for the trees encompassed by it are wanting in antiquity; and as they do not now exhibit their garden to the strangers of western and southern Europe, rumour says that they want to wait a few years till the trees grow a little. Thus do those who profess Christ's religion dishonour his name by their deceit and greed of gain, and profane this most sacred of all the places connected with his mortal career, whose situation we are able with certainty to identify.

The Latins, of course, assert that the old trees within their garden are the very trees which saw the Jews lay violent hands upon their King and their God, who walked among them in human seeming and humble guise. Travellers have remarked upon the disproportion between the huge trunks of the old olives, and their small heads and scanty foliage, which give them the appearance of having been pollarded. This characteristic may be observed to a considerable extent in the group in our illustration; but many of the oldest trees, both within and scattered around the enclosure, have this feature even more strongly marked.

In approaching Gethsemane from the bridge over the Kidron, the Chapel of the Virgin is passed, containing, according to tradition, her tomb. This stands at the northern end of a sunken court, into which a flight of steps descends at the opposite extremity. Inside the inner arch is the doorway, whence a long flight of steps leads downward to the chapel. This is excavated in the rock, and was an ancient tomb. On the right hand are shown the tombs of Joachim and Anna, the parents of the Virgin, and on the left that of Joseph, the Virgin's husband. At the extremity of the grove is a small dark chapel, containing the tomb where once the Virgin's corpse was laid. It is profusely decorated with pictures and flowers, and from the vault hang numbers of silver lamps and ornamented ostrich eggs. The front of the chapel, and its situation in the excavated court, are curious and picturesque. It is ancient and venerable in appearance, but its history is comparatively recent; for the first mention of it is by Arculfus, a French bishop, in the beginning of the eighth century. His testimony with respect to it has an additional interest, for it proves that the legend of the

Assumption of the Virgin had not been invented when he wrote: for he, as well as John the presbyter, of Damascus, who was afterwards canonized, and who wrote a few years after Arculfus, speak of the Virgin's body. The tradition which calls this cave the Virgin's tomb, and the doctrine of the Assumption, are both directly opposed to a decree of the general council held at Ephesus, A.D. 341, in which it was asserted that the Virgin and the favourite disciple St. John, to whose care she was committed by her Son, were buried in Ephesus, in the very church in which the council was then assembled. Notwithstanding this decree of a general council, and in spite of the evidence given by a bishop and by a saint, the churches both of Rome and the east have for centuries maintained that the Virgin was laid in this tomb, and then that the miracle of the Assumption took place; and they venerate this site accordingly. They are singularly unfortunate in the holy places of this underground shrine, for both Joachim and St. Anne have other tombs beneath the ancient church of St. Anne.

Monks will uphold their preposterous inventions in the face of all evidence and authority, however conclusive; and in this case one of the fraternity defended these false sepulchres on the ground that there was no reason why a person should not have two or three tombs as well as two or three houses. The traditions respecting the Assumption tell us that as the Virgin Mary mounted upwards to the sky in the presence of the disciples, St. Thomas, the incredulous, again evinced unbelief in the palpable miracle which took place before his eyes; and that, to convince him of its reality, the Virgin, as she ascended, dropped her girdle at his feet. The rock on which it fell is still supposed to retain a winding indentation, said to be the impression of the girdle miraculously made, and preserved "for the conviction of all such as shall suspect the truth of the story of the Assumption."

In the chapel of the Virgin are altars belonging to various sects; and the unseemly squabbles of modern Christians of different denominations desecrate the sacred neighbourhood of Gethsemane—the influence of whose solemn associations is powerless to check their rivalries and animosities, or to infuse some little Christian charity into their hearts.

## XII.

## THE VALLEY OF JEHOSHAPHAT.

The deep valley on the east of Jerusalem, now called the Valley of Jehoshaphat, does not appear to be mentioned by that name, either in the Old or New Testament, but is always spoken of as the Valley of the Brook Kidron. A "Valley of Jehoshaphat" is spoken of by the prophet Joel (chap. iii. 2, 12, 14): "I will gather all nations, and bring them down into the Valley of Jehoshaphat." And again: "Multitudes, multitudes in the valley of decision; for the day of the Lord is near in the valley of decision." But here no definite place is pointed out, and the word Jehoshaphat is probably used in consequence of its signification, which is "Jehovah judgeth," and refers to the judgment the Lord will execute on his enemies and the oppressors of his people. Josephus gives the name of Kidron to the valley, and we have no historical ground for giving it another name.

There certainly is an idea prevalent amongst the Roman Catholics, Jews, and Mohammedans, that this valley will be the scene of the last judgment; and in consequence of this belief all three creeds have arbitrarily given it the name of the "Valley of Jehoshaphat." This change of appellation dates from an early period of the Christian era, for the valley is so called by Eusebius and other writers of the fourth century.

When Josiah was destroying idolatry in Judah, he burned the grove sacred to Baal, and all the host of heaven, at the Brook Kidron; "and stamped it small to powder, and cast the powder thereof upon the graves of the children of the people." From this passage it would seem that a part of the valley was used as a burying-place by the Jews at a very distant period. In more modern days, it was, and still is, considered by Israel's children as the most advantageous spot in which their mortal remains can be interred. Thousands of Abraham's descendants have travelled hither from distant lands, when old age and failing strength warned them that their time on earth was short, for the sole purpose of finding graves on the eastern slope of the Valley of Jehoshaphat. All along the left bank of the ravine and up the sides of Olivet, their white tombstones are so thickly planted as in many places to resemble a pavement of thick and broad flagstones, shaken asunder and disjointed by some convulsion. Above this valley, upon the Mount of Olives, the Jews believe their Messiah will stand on the morning of the resurrection, and will summon all the dead from the dust. The mountain will be cleft asunder, and those who are buried in this favoured spot will at once rise from their tombs and instantly appear in the presence of their God and King; whilst those who have been buried in distant lands will have to make a toilsome and painful journey, burrowing like moles underground, from their far-off sepulchres, till they can emerge like the others from the earth of this valley: the surface of its soil thus becoming the portal of the resurrection through which all the dead must pass to their new life. The Moslems have adapted this tenet of the Jews to their own creed; and at the top of a lofty wall of the Haram, standing high above on the crest of the western steep, they point out a column projecting horizontally from the walls, as destined to be the throne of the prophet Mohammed on the day when he shall judge the world. There he will sit in judgment, and, according to the belief of some Moslems, from the small arched window close to his throne, a bridge no broader than a razor's edge will cross the deep glen to the opposite mountain side. Along that fearful path all mankind will have to travel. To the faithful of Islam supernatural help will be given, which will uphold them as they traverse the yawning chasm; but all who believe not in the prophet's mission will be left to their own unaided powers, their footing will fail them, and they will be precipitated into the depths of the abyss below.

The first mention of the "Brook Kidron" in Scripture is in the account of king David's flight from Jerusalem, when Absalom revolted at Hebron. "The king also himself passed over the Brook Kidron, and all the people passed over, toward the way of the wilderness." The channel of the Kidron is now, and apparently always has been, nothing more than the bed of a winter torrent. There is no continuous flow of water along its course, even in the winter; but occasionally, after violent storms of rain, a great volume of water rushes down it, for it then receives all the surface water from the sides of the neighbouring hills.

The head of the Valley of Jehoshaphat, or of the Kidron, is to the northward of Jerusalem, near the tomb of the Judges. The country here is very rocky, and there are many ancient tombs and quarries. For some distance the valley is shallow and stony; opposite the northern extremity of the city it is wide and cultivated; its sides then approach nearer, and it rapidly deepens till, just opposite the south-eastern corner of the Haram, it becomes a mere ravine between high mountains. After this, it passes the village of Siloam, there joins the Valley of Hinnom opposite the Mount of Offence, and after passing between

SILOAM FROM THE PORCH OF THE TOMB OF ST. JAMES.

that hill and the Hill of Evil Counsel, turns off almost at a right angle in a south-easterly direction, and pursues its course towards the Dead Sea. Throughout its whole extent down to this point, its rocky sides are full of excavated tombs.

The most remarkable group of these rock-hewn sepulchres is situated in the narrow ravine we have mentioned. These monuments are four in number, and are cut out of the face of the same rock. They are called the Tomb of Jehoshaphat, the Tomb or "Pillar" of Absalom, the Tomb of St. James, and the Tomb of Zacharias. The sepulchres of Absalom and Zacharias are monuments of rock standing separate from the rock out of which they have been hewn: the others are excavated chambers, with ornamental portals, in the scarped face of the cliff. The tomb of Jehoshaphat (not the king of that name, for he "was buried with his fathers in the city of David his father") is almost hidden from view, its entablature alone being visible above the rubbish heaped up at its entrance. It has a strange appearance, rising, with its richly ornamented pediment, as it were out of the heart of the mountain.

In the Scriptural account of the judgment with which God visited Absalom's unnatural rebellion, we read: "Now Absalom in his lifetime had taken and reared up for himself a pillar, which is in the king's dale; for he said, 'I have no son to keep my name in remembrance;' and he called the pillar after his own name, and it is called unto this day Absalom's Place."

The monument to which Absalom's name is now affixed has for many centuries been believed by the Jews to be the pillar mentioned in the passage of Samuel just quoted; and during all that time they have been in the habit of spitting at the monument and throwing stones at it, when they passed by, to mark their detestation of his parricidal rebellion. They also bring their children here, and tell them the story of Absalom's doom, as a warning to them to avoid Absalom's sin. The faces of the structure are scarred, and its base heaped up and encumbered with the stones that have been cast at it from time immemorial. The lower part of the pillar is cut out of the solid cliff, from which it is isolated by a broad passage excavated round it; and behind it, in one of the perpendicular faces of this area, is the portal of the tomb of Jehoshaphat, proving that the latter tomb is the most modern. It is twenty-four feet square, and is ornamented on each side with two columns and two half columns of the Ionic order, with pilasters at the corners. The architrave has Doric ornaments, and the cornice has an Egyptian character. Above this, the tomb is built of masonry of great stones, and is of singular architecture, the square edifice being surrounded by a cylinder, on the top of which is a curious concave curved pyramid, crowned by a tuft of leaves or an opening flower. The whole height is fifty-four feet. In the lower part is a small chamber eight feet square, with two recesses, each two feet deep.

Excavated in the face of the same cliff, a little further to the southward, and about fifteen feet from the ground, is the tomb of St. James. Its front is an open portal, supported by two columns and two half columns, of the Doric order, over which is a Doric frieze, with triglyphs, and a cornice. The porch is eighteen feet wide by nine deep. On the east, a plain door leads from it into the principal sepulchral chamber, whose dimensions are about seventeen feet by fourteen, from which open three smaller chambers, with recesses for bodies. On the north side of the vestibule are a door and staircase to the rock overhead; and on the south side a door and passage cut through the rock lead to the monument of Zacharias, and this is the ordinary entrance to St. James' tomb.

The tomb of Zacharias is altogether cut out of the solid rock, and is very similar in character to the pillar of Absalom, but it is surmounted by a quadrangular pyramid. The monument apparently is solid.

No one has been able to fix the age of these four tombs, or to bring forward any evidence whatever as to who may have been their tenants. There seems no probability that any one of them has a right to the name it bears. From their architecture we should conclude that they are of a later period than most of the rock-hewn sepulchres about Jerusalem. It has been suggested that the Grecian decorations may have been cut upon Absalom's original pillar, but this is mere guess-work, for we have not even the warranty of ancient tradition for its identification with that monument. It was not till the twelfth century that it was so called, and long before then it had been spoken of as the tomb of Hezekiah.

The tomb of Zacharias is said to have been erected to the memory of Zechariah, the son of Jehoiada, who was stoned by the people "at the commandment of the king, in the court of the house of the Lord," because he boldly spake God's word to them and their king Joash. But in the fourth century, the Jerusalem Itinerary calls it the tomb of Isaiah, and in the twelfth century it is described as the sepulchre of king Uzziah. The Jews, who look upon Absalom's tomb with horror, greatly reverence that of Zacharias, and prayers offered up at it are supposed to be of peculiar efficacy. Every Jew wishes to be buried as near to it as possible.

## XIII.
## CHRISTIAN ANTIQUARIES IN JERUSALEM.

The very stones of Jerusalem are dear to the Christian; but the heart of the Christian is not the only one in which Jerusalem has a place. The Jew regards her as the metropolis and the loved home of his race; and she is one of the most holy cities of the Moslem. Of late years antiquarians and archæologists have made Jerusalem and its neighbourhood one wide battle-field. Learned and pious men whose minds are stored with history, scriptural and secular, and whose hearts earnestly desire truth, view the localities of the holy city in their present state, and continually, from the same facts, arrive at conclusions strangely dissimilar.

It is cheering to the Christian's heart, among all these conflicts of the zealous and the learned, among all the claims put forward, whether by the simple and credulous or by the interested and knavish, to light upon some spot concerning which no rational doubt can exist; to feel certain that we are on the real scene where Christ wrought one of his miracles, and that Jesus the God-man, who worked such wonders and endured such sufferings for us, really stood where we stand and looked upon what we now see. The learned may dispute about Akra and Bezetha, the limits of the third wall, and the course of the famous "Valley of the Cheesemongers;" yet we can trust to the great leading features which God's hand stamped upon the land at its creation, and we can surely identify Zion, Moriah, Olivet, Gihon, Hinnom, and the Kidron; we can but guess at the northern boundary of the city, but we know to within a few yards where the Redeemer prayed and his disciples slumbered in Gethsemane.

Many places have for fifteen centuries borne titles conferred on them by the early Christians; and others, more recently dignified by a sacred connexion, are called by no other names than those which have been erroneously given them. The tomb of St. James, for instance, does not pretend to have ever held his corpse, but it received its name from a traditional incident in his history which may never have occurred. It is related that when St. James saw the Redeemer dead upon the cross, he called to mind our Lord's predictions about his resurrection, and with an active faith in his Master's words, he vowed that he would neither eat nor drink till he should see his Lord risen again from the grave. In the recesses of this tomb he hid himself till the third day. Then as he was with the other apostles, our Lord appeared and said, "Arise and eat; for I am now risen from the dead."

From the fourth century, when foreign ecclesiastics crowded to Jerusalem, and appended Scriptural names and Bible stories to every monument about the holy city, the traditions respecting the particular group described in the last chapter seem to have continually varied. We have mentioned that the two monoliths called after Absalom and Zacharias are spoken of in the Jerusalem Itinerary (A.D. 333) as dedicated to Isaiah and Hezekiah; but Adamnanus, about A.D. 697, calls one the tomb of Jehoshaphat, and says that the two excavated sepulchres near it were those of Simeon the Just and Joseph the husband of the Virgin Mary.

The view engraved in the last chapter is taken from the interior of the vestibule of the so-called tomb or cave of St. James, looking down the valley of Jehoshaphat towards the village of Siloam. Nearer to us, the dark hill face of Mount Moriah descends to the bed of the Kidron, which is hidden by an intervening brow thickly studded with Jewish gravestones. This burial-place is of more modern date than that upon the hill above the monuments, and is called "The House of the Living." It was almost a matter of course that the monks would connect some spots in the vicinity of Jerusalem with the memory of St. James, the son of Zebedee; but we have no trustworthy evidence in favour of the authenticity of the reputed site of his martyrdom, nor does the legend of the cave rest on good authority.

Descending the Valley of Jehoshaphat we come to the Fountain of the Virgin called by the Arabs, "The Fountain of the Mother of Steps." Nothing in the neighbourhood of Jerusalem bears more distinctly the traces of high antiquity than does the approach to this spring. The water rises at the bottom of an artificial cavern twenty-five feet deep. Descending a flight of steps, a large arched chamber is reached, from whence another flight of steps leads down to a rude cave where the water issues from the rock. The fountain is remittent, and at irregular intervals the water suddenly rises in the cave and flows off through its underground channel with a much stronger current, and, after a few minutes perhaps, it suddenly ebbs. In summer, sometimes the spring is dry, and the people who draw their supplies from it wait around with their thirsty animals, until suddenly the water bubbles up and gives a plentiful stream. Possibly this may have been the Pool of Bethesda, the scene of our Lord's miracle upon the impotent man. An underground channel conducts the water from this fountain to the Pool of Siloam, engraved in this chapter.

THE POOL OF SILOAM.

## XIV.

## THE WATERS OF SILOAM AND THE KING'S GARDEN.

The "Fountain of the Virgin" is so called from a tradition that the Virgin Mary, before her purification, there washed the clothes of the infant Jesus. It is also called the "Fountain of Accused Women," from a story that women used to be made to drink its waters as a kind of ordeal. If guilty, they died the moment they tasted it.

As long ago as the beginning of the seventeenth century, it was known that the waters of this fountain were carried off by an excavated channel, and of late the current belief was that they supplied the Pool of Siloam. Dr. Robinson, and his companion, Mr. Eli Smith, set this question at rest. They first entered the tunnel, through which water flows into the Pool of Siloam, and made their way along its course for a distance of eight hundred feet. For the first hundred feet the passage was from fifteen to twenty feet high, for another hundred feet it was from six to ten feet in height; then it sank to four feet, and gradually became lower and lower till the explorers found they could only proceed by crawling on all-fours through the water. As they were not dressed in a costume that made this mode of progress convenient, they desisted from their attempt for the time, and having traced their initials and the figures 800 with the smoke of their candles on the roof, they retraced their steps. A few days afterwards they returned to the pool, and proceeding above ground, measured its distance from the fountain, and found it to be eleven hundred feet; and as they had already traversed more than two-thirds of that distance under ground, they commenced operations this time at the Fountain of the Virgin, hoping that their subterranean journey would not exceed three hundred, or, at most, four hundred feet. They descended to the fountain, and there taking off their clothes, dressed themselves in wide Arab drawers, and entered the channel on all-fours; but it became so low that they could only get forward by lying down at full length and dragging themselves along by their elbows. They came to many turns and zigzags, and places where the workmen had cut forward for some distance; and then, finding that they had left the right direction, had gone back and begun again at a different angle. The explorers went on so long that they feared they were pursuing a channel which did not communicate with the one which they had previously entered; but at length, to their great relief, after having crept along in an extremely cramped and fatiguing attitude for nine hundred and fifty feet, they came to their former mark on the roof of the channel, and proved the existence of a passage between the Fountain of the Virgin and the Pool of Siloam, and that the popular surmise was well founded. The whole passage is cut out of the solid rock, and is seventeen hundred and fifty feet long. Its width throughout is two feet. It is evident that workmen began to excavate at both ends, and met somewhere in the middle; and the reason why the channel is so much more lofty at the lower end seems to be that the workmen there began at too high a level, and when they met the shaft from the other side, finding that the water would not flow all the way, they then cut down the lower end till the stream ran through. The descent is but slight, and the water flows smoothly and softly down it to the Pool of Siloam.

It is supposed that the head of the spring, whose waters are first seen at the Fountain of the Virgin, is somewhere beneath the area of the Temple on Moriah; but the inclosure of the Moslem Haram is forbidden ground to Christian topographists, so that, at present, the source of the stream must remain a secret to us. Its outlet, however, where in the Pool of Siloam it first sees the light of day, was sanctified by one of the most important miracles wrought by our Lord upon earth.

The last day—the great day—of the feast of Tabernacles was ended, and "Jesus went unto the Mount of Olives; and early in the morning he came again into the Temple, and all the people came unto him, and he sat down and taught them," until at last the Jews, blinded by fanaticism, took up stones to cast at him. Jesus then going through the midst of them so passed by; and as he passed by, he saw a man who was blind from his birth, not because of his own or his parents' sin, but because it was predestined that in his person God was to be glorified. The "Light of the World" anointed the blind man's eyes, and said, "Go, wash in the Pool of Siloam (which is by interpretation, Sent). He went his way therefore and washed, and came seeing." Scarcely was his natural sight restored, before temptation assailed him and persecution threatened him; but spiritual eyesight was given to him strong and clear by the same Power that had wrought the more palpable miracle, and in the strength of his faith and gratitude he boldly testified before men, and, careless of consequences, openly proclaimed that from God alone could have come such a cure as his. The new convert was cast out of the synagogue; but Jesus found him, and guided to a more accurate and complete knowledge of himself his young disciple's earnest trust and fearless zeal. The man whose eyes were so lately opened, saw and

THE KING'S GARDEN.

talked with Jesus his benefactor; and then, in full belief that he was in very truth the Son of God, he worshipped him.

More than eighteen centuries have flown since in Siloam's pool the blind man washed from his eyes the clay placed there by the finger of his Saviour; and in that very pool, in water flowing from its ancient source, the traveller may dip his hands and drink. Of the identity of the pool, supplied by the conduit described above, with the scene of the miracle, there is no doubt whatever. Josephus often mentions the fountain of Siloam, and tells us its exact situation in the mouth of the valley of the Tyropœon. The Jerusalem Itinerary, A.D. 333, speaks of the pool and its position. Jerome describes the locality of the pool, and is the first writer who alludes to the irregular flow of its waters. Antoninus Martyr in the seventh century, the monk Bernard in the ninth, and the historians of the Crusades, place the pool or fountain of Siloam in its present site. William of Tyre mentions its intermittent flow, and others speak of it both as a fountain and a pool. Phocas, in A.D. 1185, says the fountain was surrounded by arches and massive columns with gardens below. Not till the end of the fifteenth century is there any reference to the Fountain of the Virgin, and only in the eighteenth century was it called the Fountain of Siloam; so that what we call the Pool of Siloam is what is alluded to by all the early writers, either by that name or as the Fountain of Siloam.

The Pool of Siloam is about fifty-five feet long, and twenty feet deep. Its masonry is comparatively modern. The columns, partly built into the sides, are ancient, and probably supported a roof; and perhaps arches may have sprung from them, so as to form porches, similar to those which we read existed at the Pool of Bethesda. The arched entrance at the upper end of the pool leads by a ruinous staircase down to the conduit by which it is supplied.

During the Feast of Tabernacles, water mingled with wine was poured out upon the sacrifice which lay ready prepared upon the altar, in the Temple. This water was drawn by one of the priests in a golden vessel from the Pool of Siloam, and at night took place "the rejoicing for the drawing of water"— a festival which lasted till far into the night; and it is said, "This their rejoicing was of so high a jollity, that he that never saw the rejoicing for the drawing of water, never saw rejoicing all his life." "Rabbi Levi saith: 'Why is the name of it called the drawing of water? Because of the pouring out of the Holy Ghost, according to what is said, With joy shall ye draw water out of the wells of salvation.'" "The cast-off breeches and belts of the priests were torn into shreds for wicks: there was not a court in Jerusalem that was not illuminated by the lights of the water drawing."

It seems probable that our Lord alluded to this ceremony of the drawing of water from the Pool of Siloam, when in the Temple on the last and great day of the Feast of Tabernacles he "stood and cried, saying, If any man thirst, let him come unto me and drink. He that believeth on me, as the Scripture hath said, Out of his belly shall flow rivers of living water."

The water from the Pool of Siloam flows down to the King's Garden, the greenest and most productive spot around Jerusalem. Nehemiah mentions this place, and says that Shallum built "the wall of the pool of Siloah by the king's garden;" and here it was that when David was old and stricken in years, Adonijah, one of the very goodly sons born to him in Hebron, called together and feasted the king's sons, and the men of Judah, the king's servants; and here they proclaimed him king. But not even the help of the mighty Joab could give Adonijah his father's throne; and hither from Zion was borne the sound of shouting, which broke in upon their banquet. David had named Solomon as his successor; and Solomon rode on David's mule, and they blew the trumpet, and all the people said, God save king Solomon, and rejoiced with great joy, so that the earth rent with the sound of them. Then the guests, who had just "made an end of eating" at the feast in the king's delicious gardens, "were afraid, and rose up, and went every man his way."

We have given a view taken from the King's Garden, looking up the Valley of Jehoshaphat. On the right is the village of Siloam, whose inhabitants cultivate the rich garden below. The south-eastern point of Moriah, crowned by the mosque of Aksa and the wall of the Haram, closes the view up the valley. It was up the steep of Moriah that Adonijah fled, when his fair-weather friends had deserted him; and within the sacred enclosure on its crest, he caught hold on the horns of the altar for safety.

## XV.
## THE WATERS OF JERUSALEM.

The Moslems have a great veneration for the Fountain of Siloam, and Mohammed is reported to have declared, "Zemzem and Siloam are two fountains of Paradise." In ancient times the waters of Siloam were more abundant than they are now, and their flow and ebb, both in the Fountain of the Virgin and the Pool of Siloam, were more remarkable. The surplus water from this pool seems to have supplied another reservoir before it reached the King's Garden, for a causeway crosses the valley of the Tyropæon, acting as a dam; and above it the ground is lower and forms a kind of basin, now cultivated as a garden.

Just above the causeway is a curious old mulberry tree, whose ancient roots are protected by stones and earth heaped up round them. This aged tree marks the traditional scene of Isaiah's martyrdom. According to the rabbins, the prophet was sawn asunder in the trunk of a tree, during the reign of Manasseh, Hezekiah's evil son. Probably this took place soon after Manasseh's accession; for at that time Isaiah, who had prophesied during the four preceding reigns, must have been stricken in years, three of the monarchs throughout whose reigns he ministered having together ruled for sixty-one years. The tree is spoken of as of immense age, by a writer in the sixteenth century.

In all ages the city of Jerusalem had an abundant supply of water within its walls, and in all the sieges to which it was subjected we nowhere find any mention of a want of water in the city. During the siege by Titus, when Jerusalem was crowded with strangers in addition to its permanent inhabitants, and the Jews were dying of hunger in thousands daily, there is not a word said of any want of water. The neighbourhood of the city was almost arid; and though there is no instance on record of the besieged having suffered from thirst, the besiegers on many occasions were greatly distressed by drought. During the siege by Antiochus Pius, the operations were much delayed by this cause, and Josephus regards it as the result of a Divine interposition that the Romans under Titus were not likewise reduced to great straits. It has been suggested, however, that the language of Josephus respecting the plentiful supply of water procured by the Romans from Siloam, may have been only a boast to deceive the Jews; for Dio relates that the legions suffered frightfully from thirst, and were obliged to bring bad water from a distance. The Crusaders were reduced to the greatest extremities by thirst during their siege in the summer of A.D. 1099, whilst the inhabitants were well supplied; and in every age the truth of the short description of the city given by Strabo has been demonstrated: "Jerusalem, a rocky well-enclosed fortress; within well watered, without wholly dry."

At present the chief water supply of Jerusalem is derived from cisterns, and to a great extent this must always have been the case. Almost every tolerable private house has one or more of these cisterns, which are excavated in the limestone rock, and many of them are of enormous size. The greater part of these are ancient, and their number and extent afford a conclusive reason why the Jews never experienced any want of water during a siege. The springs in and about Jerusalem are few, and not very copious at the present day. In the time of Hezekiah, they seemed to have given a more liberal flow, for we read that when Sennacherib threatened Jerusalem, the first defensive operation undertaken by the king was this: "He took counsel with his princes and his mighty men to stop the waters of the fountains which were without the city, and they did help him. So there was gathered much people together, who stopped all the fountains, and the brook that ran through the midst of the land, saying, Why should the kings of Assyria come and find much water?" We afterwards read that, "This same Hezekiah also stopped the upper water-courses of Gihon, and brought it straight down to the west side of the city of David;" also, "He made a pool and a conduit, and brought water into the city." In Ecclesiasticus also it is stated, that "he brought in water into the midst of the city; he dug with iron into the rock." He probably covered over the spring of Gihon in subterranean chambers of the same kind as those above Solomon's Pool, so as to hide it from an invader, and then carried the water by channels underground into reservoirs constructed in the city.

The picturesque pool which still bears, and probably with reason, Hezekiah's name is at present about two hundred and forty feet long, and one hundred and fifty feet broad; but it appears originally to have extended about fifty-seven feet further towards the north, and thus to have been about a hundred yards long. The subterranean channel which was discovered in digging the foundations for the English church, is probably Hezekiah's conduit.

Beneath the area of the Haram, the site of the Temple, ancient writers tell us that a vast system of waterworks existed: one cistern or rather series of cisterns constructed by the high priest Simon the Just, the son of Onias, in the

ENTRANCE TO THE TOMBS OF THE JUDGES.

reign of Ptolemy Soter in Egypt, was "in compass as the sea," covered with plates of brass. Aristeas, too, a writer who visited Jerusalem about A.D. 273, in the reign of Soter's successor, speaks of a never-failing fountain beneath the Temple area, and of these reservoirs; and says that their floors and sides were cased with lead, and that there were hidden apertures, known only to those employed at the sacrifices, through which the water gushing out with force washed off all the blood of the numerous victims. To some other great reservoirs here the water was brought from Solomon's Pool; and all accounts agree that many cisterns of marvellous capacity existed beneath the Temple platform. A vast vault, called the cistern of Helena, cut entirely out of the solid rock, now belongs to the convent of the Copts; there is another in the church of the Flagellation, and a third near the Damascus gate; another of huge dimensions in the Latin convent is able in seasons of drought to supply all the Christian inhabitants of the city; and there are many others.

It has always been believed that, in addition to its supplies from Solomon's Pool, and from rain water, a strong spring existed beneath the Temple area; but at present Moslem bigotry is a bar to all investigation. Just outside the sacred enclosure is a well, called the "Well of the Bath," supposed to be connected with the waters of the Haram. This was partially explored by Mr. Wolcott, an American missionary. At the dead of night, attended only by a servant lad, and furnished with candles, matches, a measuring rule, and a compass, he went to the well's mouth. Here he met two peasants who had been induced by the keeper of the bath to aid the enterprise, and by them he was lowered to the bottom of the well. A leaky leathern bucket had been tied as a counterpoise to the other end of the rope by which he was suspended, and after meeting it half way down, he was under a shower-bath for the rest of his descent. The well was eighty-three feet deep, and the water in it about four feet and a half. The well's mouth was only two feet square, but it soon expanded to twelve feet square. Six feet above the water he found a doorway leading into an arched chamber, which he contrived to reach. He here relit his candles, which had been extinguished. The chamber was fifteen feet by ten, and did not seem to have been constructed with any reference to the water. Opposite to the chamber was a passage which formed the water channel. Mr. Wolcott descended into the water, having first put on an india-rubber life preserver, and then followed the passage, which was about ten feet high, till he came to another vault, twenty feet square, beyond which the passage was about five feet high and was covered with stones, among which were fragments of marble and granite columns. Having followed this passage for eighty feet, he was stopped by a well of unknown depth, on the opposite side of which the wall of rock descended to the water and stopped further progress. It has been supposed from the accounts given by the attendants at the bath, who, when the water was low, had visited the well which stopped Mr. Wolcott's explorations, that from it there is a continuation of the water passage at a lower level, and that this lower gallery communicates with the Haram. Mr. Wolcott deserves great credit for his intrepidity; for had there been the least alarm during his descent or ascent, the peasants would have let the rope slip, and have fled from the spot; and had they even run off while he was exploring the water channel, his position would have been neither pleasant nor safe; for, first, he would have had to attract attention and induce somebody to draw him up; and when he reappeared on the surface of the earth, he would have had to give an explanation which should prove satisfactory to savage fanatics as to how he chanced to be wandering underground so near to the limits of their sacred shrines. The whole story is a good illustration of the difficulties thrown in the way of the Christian antiquary by the intolerant infidels who rule the city of David and of Christ; and till free scope is given to examine, and where necessary to make excavations, the source whence much of that extraordinary amount of water which filled the pools and vaulted reservoirs of Jerusalem, and especially of the Temple, was drawn, must remain a mystery.

The quantity in the covered cisterns alone must have been far beyond the ordinary wants of the population, and they had many vast pools as well, both within and without the walls. The position of the Pool of Bethesda has not been determined. The monks have identified the enormous reservoir just within St. Stephen's Gate with the pool of the five porches, where on the sabbath day Jesus wrought a good and merciful work upon a man who for thirty-eight years had been weighed down with infirmity. Some modern authorities believe that this great trench to the north of the Haram was the scene of the miracle just alluded to, but evidence to connect them is wanting. The excavation is very remarkable. At present it is three hundred and sixty feet long, a hundred and thirty feet broad, and seventy-five feet deep; but it was anciently much deeper, for the bottom is covered to a considerable depth by the rubbish of centuries. It is coated with cement, and has evidently been used as a reservoir.

In this chapter a view is given of the entrance to the Tombs of the Judges on the north side of Jerusalem, to be described afterwards.

## XVI.
## THE VALLEY OF THE SON OF HINNOM.

The holy city stands upon a broad and lofty promontory formed by two valleys which at their commencement to the northward of the city are shallow, but grow deeper and narrower as they descend, until sweeping round the south-eastern and south-western steeps of Moriah and Zion they become wild ravines, craggy and precipitous, and finally unite to the south of the city. On the east, west, and south, these two valleys were the natural boundaries of ancient Jerusalem, and its natural protection. The ancient walls of Jerusalem from the time of Solomon to that of Titus, must have taken their course along the declivities girded round by these ravines. Whether they were built along the crest of the hill, or whether they and the city they defended came far down the slope, we cannot now decide; but we know for certain that these two glens were in fact a tremendous ditch limiting and defending one of the strongest fortresses in the world. One of these valleys is the Valley of the Kidron or of Jehoshaphat, whose course we have already described; the other is the Valley of Hinnom. A third valley, much smaller, and of less depression, divides the elevated platform on which Jerusalem stands, and passing between Zion and Moriah, dips down to meet the other two glens at their point of junction, and, uniting with them, passes southward between the Mountain of Offence on the east and the Hill of Evil Counsel on the west, eventually to fall with them into the Dead Sea. This third valley is the Tyropœon.

The "Valley of Hinnom," or the "Valley of the Son of Hinnom," as it is more commonly designated in the Old Testament, is called in Hebrew "Ge Hinnom," and from its Jewish name it is called by the Arabs "Wady Jehennam." This valley begins to the westward of Jerusalem. Its upper part is a shallow basin, and in the centre of this basin is the large reservoir called the Upper Pool of Gihon, and by the Arabs Birket el Mamilla. From hence the valley, which is from fifty to a hundred yards wide, runs almost south-east till it nears the Jaffa gate, when it turns almost due south, and grows deeper. About a quarter of a mile below the Jaffa gate is the lower pool of Gihon, called in Arabic "Birket es Sultân." This pool was formed by throwing strong walls across the bottom of the valley, between which the earth was wholly removed, so that the rocky sides of the valley are left shelving down irregularly, and form a narrow channel along the middle. Walls run along the sides, but these, as well as the northern dam, are ruinous. At the south end the wall forms a broad causeway, crossed by a road. The length of the pool is nearly six hundred feet. Its breadth at the northern end is two hundred and forty-five feet, and at the southern end two hundred and seventy-five feet, and its depth at this lower end forty-two feet. This pool is usually dry.

Just above this lower pool, the aqueduct from Solomon's Pool crosses the valley upon nine low arches. An Arabic inscription says that it was "built" by an Egyptian sultan about A.D. 1300, which no doubt means that he repaired it at that date. In this part of the valley the city wall high overhead has a very picturesque effect. The glen soon turns eastward, and runs in an easterly direction till it joins the Valley of Jehoshaphat; and this lower portion is very stern and wild, the declivity of Zion on the north falling steeply into it, and the hill on the south rising in broken irregular cliffs, honeycombed with tombs. This valley, especially the deep retired glen towards its lower end, has an awful notoriety, for this is Tophet; and here it was that the children of Judah did evil in the sight of the Lord, and built the high places of Tophet, "which is in the Valley of the Son of Hinnom, to burn their sons and daughters in the fire. Therefore behold the days come, saith the Lord, that it shall no more be called Tophet, nor the Valley of the Son of Hinnom, but the Valley of Slaughter; for they shall bury in Tophet till there be no place."

It was king Solomon the wise who wrought the folly which brought a curse and defilement upon this wild valley, for he loved strange women of the nations concerning which the Lord said unto the children of Israel, "Ye shall not go in to them, neither shall they come in unto you; for surely they will turn away your heart after their gods."

With his command to his people in this instance, the Almighty deigned to give a reason for his prohibition. High and low in Israel disobeyed this injunction; and, as a notable example to the whole people of the weakness of man when he acts without reference to God's laws, and his helplessness to resist temptation, the God of Abraham chose out the ruler of Israel, the wisest of mankind, and giving him over to his own devices, permitted him publicly to work foolishness in Israel. Wise Solomon, when he disobeyed God, was led astray by the strange wives to whom his heart clave; and on the "Mount of Corruption," or "Offence," "the hill that is before Jerusalem," on the brow looking up the Valley of Hinnom, and in full view of the glorious Temple he had raised to the living God, he in his old age built a high place for Chemosh,

MORIAH AND THE VALLEY OF JEHOSHAPHAT, FROM THE MOUNT OF OFFENCE.

the abomination of Moab, and for Molech, the abomination of the children of Ammon. For this idolatry, ten tribes were taken from David's house, and for David's sake alone was there a remnant left to his posterity.

From time to time, in close vicinity to the spot where Solomon transgressed, the horrible rites of the false gods were revived by Judah's idolatrous kings. When the hill of Zion blazed gloriously in the refulgence of the setting sun, its shadow fell dark and cold upon this extremity of the Vale of Hinnom; and here within the very shade of the holy hill of Zion, did Ahaz burn his children in the flames in sacrifice to the foul gods of fire. From hence, and from the hills around, the smoke of incense burning in honour of the abominations of the heathen ascended to the sky, in defiance of the Lord of Hosts. The evil king Manasseh, too, in every respect followed in his grandfather's footsteps, and like him perpetrated in this place deeds of savage cruelty and wickedness. According to the rabbins, the statue of Molech which stood here was of brass, having the body of a man and the head of an ox. The interior was hollow and fitted up with a large furnace, by which the whole statue was easily made red-hot. The children to be sacrificed were then placed in its arms, while drums were beaten to drown their cries. Many a Jewish mother in this shady glen, with broken heart, pressed for the last time her infant to her breast; then it was torn from her loving grasp and committed to the deadly embrace of the hideous brazen monster, while the rattle of drums, the clang of cymbals, and the shouts of the frenzied idolaters, prevented a single shriek from reaching even a mother's ear. Such was the worship wise Solomon inaugurated on the rock above; and there, and in the valley below, it continued till the days of Josiah.

Josiah defiled Tophet and the high places which were on the right hand of the Mount of Corruption, which Solomon the king had builded. He polluted the scenes of heathen worship by spreading human bones and other corruptions over them, thus making Tophet ceremonially unclean, so that no Jew could enter it. Most commentators assert that perpetual fires were here kept up for consuming the bodies of criminals, carcases of animals, and other unclean things that were combustible; but this view admits of doubt. The acts of Josiah in making this valley unclean to the Jews caused the words of Jeremiah to be literally fulfilled; for tombs in multitudes have perforated all the cliffs, and we have spoken already of the crowded burying ground in the Valley of Jehoshaphat. When Titus took the city, the Valley of the Son of Hinnom was indeed a "valley of slaughter," for Josephus relates that when the victor saw these valleys below Jerusalem heaped full of dead bodies, he raised his hands and called Heaven to witness that he was not responsible for this frightful slaughter. Close to Tophet, on a sort of ledge half way up the side of the Hill of Evil Counsel, is the reputed site of Aceldama, " the Field of Blood," bought with the thirty pieces of silver, the price of our Lord's betrayal—the potter's field bought with the price of him who was valued, to bury strangers in. From the age of Jerome till the present time every writer on Jerusalem refers to this spot as undoubtedly the potter's field; and it is most probable that in the fourth century the field especially bought to bury strangers in would be known.

On the summit of the hill above, that awful bargain is said to have been struck; and the "Hill of Evil Counsel" takes its name from the evil consultation between the traitor who sold, and the bigots who bought, as to the best means of carrying out their purposed treachery and violence; for on the summit of this hill the country house of Caiaphas is said to have stood; and thither tradition reports that Judas went to sell his Lord. The ruins, apparently of an Arab village, are dignified by the monks with the name of the Villa of Caiaphas, and a solitary tree of peculiar shape and blasted appearance is, according to the latest ecclesiastical authorities, the very tree whose boughs aided Judas in his self-murder. Early writers place the "Field of Blood" where Judas died at different places in the Valley of Jehoshaphat.

Aceldama, the potter's field, is not marked by any boundary to distinguish it from the rest of the hill-side; and the ancient charnel house, now a ruin, is all that remains to point out the site. It is a long, massive stone building, in front of a cave in the face of a precipice. The roof is arched, the walls sunk deep below the level of the ground outside, and the earth inside removed, leaving a huge pit, twenty feet deep. Through a hole the bottom can be seen, over which bones were scattered.

The potter's field, bought to bury strangers in, was used for this its original purpose by the Latins and then by the Crusaders; for here they buried pilgrims. Sir John Maundeville, in the fourteenth century, says that "in that feld ben manye tombes of Cristene men; for there ben manye pilgrymes graven."

The first mention of the Valley of the Son of Hinnom is in the book of Joshua, where it is spoken of as forming the boundary line between the portions of Judah and Benjamin. Afterwards it is always mentioned in connexion with the abominable idolatries there perpetrated, which brought down God's judgments upon those who practised them.

In this chapter is given a view of the *eastern* half of Jerusalem, as seen from the Mount of Offence. The next chapter will contain the *western* half of this prospect, with the description of the whole.

## XVII.
## THE MOUNTAIN OF THE LORD'S HOUSE.

We have now described the two valleys which gave its distinctive character to the situation of Jerusalem. The first has been fixed on by superstition as the scene of the last judgment. The name of the latter, Ge Hinnom, or Gehenna, from its ceremonial defilement and from the abominable fire of Molech which had desecrated it, was used by the later Jews to denote the place of eternal punishment. Some of the rabbins look upon it as the mouth of hell. Thus the Valley of Hinnom became the image of the place of everlasting punishment, "where their worm dieth not, and the fire is not quenched;" and the word Gehenna is thus used by our blessed Lord on many occasions.

Just below the junction of the two valleys is a well, called by the Arabs "Bir Eyûb," the well of Job or of Joab; and by the Jews and Franks, the well of Nehemiah. This well has been identified with Enrogel, a landmark of the boundary between Judah and Benjamin; and the balance of evidence seems to favour this view, though some respectable authorities dissent from it.

It was at Enrogel that Jonathan and Ahimaaz, David's servants, waited for information and advice from Hushai, who during Absalom's rebellion remained in the city, in order that by his means God might defeat the good counsel of the wise Ahithophel, and bring evil on the parricidal rebel. There are indications still extant which show that the gardens watered by Siloam extended to this well, and it was near Enrogel that Adonijah's feast in the king's garden took place.

The well is a hundred and twenty-five feet deep, walled up with large squared stones, and is apparently of great antiquity. Usually the water in it is about fifty feet deep, but in the rainy season it becomes quite full, and sometimes overflows.

Ascending the Mount of Offence, from thence may be scanned the broad prospect of Jerusalem outspread before the eyes. It is one of especial interest, for probably more than any other, except the birds-eye view from Olivet, it comprehends the leading features of the city, and shows us their relative positions. A truthful representation of the whole extent of the city, as seen from the south-east could not be given in one engraving: the sketch is therefore divided in half; but in the description we shall treat it as a whole, as by so doing our readers will be better able to form an accurate idea both of the ancient position and present appearance of the city. We shall consequently speak of the two engravings as united in one.

On the extreme right of the view, the steeps of Olivet descend into the Valley of Jehoshaphat, whose entire course along the eastern side of the city we here see. Just beneath the tower, standing near the base of that sacred hillside, are a grove of olives and a portion of a line of wall. There is Gethsemane. Nearer to us, just seen above the lower brow of the hill on which we stand, are the two monolithic monuments attributed to Absalom and Zacharias, with a portion of the scarped rock from which they were hewn, and in whose face the tombs of Jehoshaphat and St. James are excavated. Cresting the declivity which faces the Mount of Olives, at its furthest point from us, a line of towers is seen extending to the north-eastern corner of the present city, and above the houses in this quarter we can see the line of battlements of the northern wall running directly to the west. At the point in the eastern wall, where there is a break in the regular succession of the towers mentioned above, stands St. Stephen's Gate; and from that gate, which is hidden from us by a bend in the wall, the path which leads over the bridge of the Kidron to the Mount of Olives and to Bethany is seen winding down the steep descent.

A little within St. Stephen's Gate, the minaret which towers above the houses and breaks the outline of the northern wall behind, stands close to the great trench called by the monks the Pool of Bethesda, but which was probably the ditch of the splendid fortress Antonia; and this marks the northern limit of the great platform of the Haram enclosure. The wall from St. Stephen's Gate down to the lofty corner nearest to us forms the eastern boundary of the Haram; and from that corner, and past the spot where the modern line of fortification descends the hill, to the end of the high wall beyond, is the southern face of the sacred enclosure, and on the west it is bounded by the valley of the Tyropœon. This is Moriah. Upon this mount it is supposed that Abraham built the altar to sacrifice his son; and here he won the blessing which had its partial fruition in the gorgeous pile raised by his descendant on the spot hallowed by the patriarch's act of implicit obedience to God's command. Upon this mount undoubtedly stood the threshing-floor of Ornan the Jebusite. There, without doubt, Solomon built the Temple of the Most High, the richest building the world ever saw; and within the sacred area whose limits we have described, Jesus, a child of twelve years old, for the first time put his hand to his "Father's

ZION AND THE NORTHERN SLOPE OF HINNOM, FROM THE MOUNT OF OFFENCE.

business," and seated amongst the learned and the aged of Israel's doctors, within God's glorious house, discussed with them the things of God. Here, when grown to man's estate, and in the performance of his earthly mission, Christ "taught daily" and "preached the gospel;" here, too, he spoke the prophecy so literally fulfilled, that in the evil days to come, every goodly stone of God's own sanctuary should be disjointed and overthrown; and here also he foretold the prostration of "the temple of his body," and of its glorious renewal when on the third day the bonds of death were broken. Here when the Lord was taken from the apostles up to his Father and their Father, Peter wrought a miracle in Jesus' name, and preached the faith of Jesus dead and risen. Hither came the apostles, miraculously released by God's angel from their prison; and here Paul was seized by the people who went about to kill him.

The vast platform on Moriah's summit possesses an overpowering interest for us, for it is one of the few relics which tell of Israel's glory. The massive walls that bound it on the east, south, and west, are identical with and stand upon the very substructure of the outer wall of the ancient temple. Many portions of this substructure certainly belonged to Nehemiah's temple, and probably to that of Solomon. It is at the south-eastern angle, the lofty corner just opposite to us, that the old stones of Jerusalem standing in their original position, standing as when our Lord looked on them, are best seen. Here, fifteen or sixteen courses of the grand old blocks, beautifully cut and bevelled, still remain, and many more must be covered with rubbish. This grand fragment of Jewish workmanship forms perhaps one of the finest specimens of mural architecture in the world. The chief corner stones are twenty feet long, and the eighth, counting upwards, is seven feet broad and six feet high. The length of the stones in all this old Jewish work varies much; the greatest length of any single block now above-ground in this place is twenty-three feet. The Jews seem to have bestowed especial care upon the corners of their buildings, which everywhere exhibit a greater degree of finish, and a better choice of material than the plain wall, fine as its masonry may be.

At the south-western angle, which, owing to gardens, thickets of cactus, and dirt, is not so accessible as the corner we have described, the stones of the Jewish substructure are still grander in their dimensions; and here the lowest corner stone above ground is thirty-one feet long and six feet and a half broad. Other stones are from twenty to twenty-five feet long and five feet high. About a dozen yards from this angle, Dr. Robinson discovered the segment of a gigantic arch projecting from the wall. Now this arch is certainly as ancient as any of the Jewish remains here, and in every respect its position corresponds with that of the bridge which, according to Josephus, connected the Temple with the upper city of Zion. Whether this was the ascent by which Solomon went up into the house of the Lord - one of those items of the monarch's magnificence which when the queen of Sheba saw "there was no more spirit in her," or whether it belongs to a later epoch, we have not space to discuss. The valley of the Tyropæon, which was spanned by this bridge, has been gradually filled up by ruin and rubbish, to what depth is unknown, and excavations here would most likely lead to valuable discoveries. The western wall has a greater proportion of ancient Jewish workmanship than either of the others; but much of it is hidden in the fronts of Turkish houses built up against it.

The "mountain of the Lord's house" has greatly changed in outward shape since David bought the threshing-floor of Ornan. At that time it was surmounted by a mass of limestone rock, with precipitous sides, from which the ground fell rapidly to the valleys of the Kidron and the Tyropæon on the east and west, and to the lower brow of Ophel on the south. Ornan's threshing-floor probably was the only level space on its summit. The broad platform we see is almost entirely artificial. Upon the rocky crown of Moriah, which seems to have been cut down to form a larger level, Solomon placed the fane and altar. On the east he built a wall lower down the hill, and filled the intervening hollow with earth, on which he erected a covered colonnade. Afterwards, the level area was extended on the other sides by the same process, the space within the walls being partly filled in with earth and partly supported upon piers and arches.

Thus was formed the Court of the Gentiles. Porticoes ran along the outer walls of the enclosure, and the open part was paved with variegated stones. Here, both Jews and strangers spent much of their leisure, and trade at last encroached upon the sacred precincts. Then it was that our Saviour drove out from this outer court the buyers and sellers who profaned it by carrying on there their secular business, which was not untainted by fraud. The eastern colonnade was called Solomon's Porch, and there Jesus often walked. Along the southern side extended the noble cloister of Herod, one of the most remarkable of his magnificent works; and its position, stretching from valley to valley along the summit of the massive wall, must have rendered it an object of striking grandeur from almost every point of view in and around the city. It consisted of four rows of Corinthian columns, forming a central nave and two side aisles. Each aisle was thirty feet in width and fifty in height, while the nave was forty-five feet wide and a hundred feet high. The columns were of white marble and the roofs of cedar.

## XVIII.
## EL HARAM ESH-SHERIF, OR THE NOBLE SANCTUARY.

HAVING spoken of the vaults, cisterns, and water-works below the platform of the Haram, the more noted objects of attention aboveground will now be alluded to briefly. Though there are many theories respecting it, only one of them seems to be satisfactory. It appears to be almost certain that the Haram area, shut in on three sides by the walls described in the last chapter, and on the fourth, the northern extremity, by the deep trench at St. Stephen's Gate and by the governor's house, is identical with the space covered by the Jewish Temple, including the fortress of Antonia. In our Saviour's time, Solomon's Temple was but a tradition; the Temple of Zerubbabel had been altogether reconstructed, and the Temple so often mentioned in the New Testament, and described by Josephus and the rabbinical writers, was the building raised by Herod the Great. This was a strong fortress, and Antonia was its citadel.

The sacred enclosure of the Haram, from the day when the Crusaders were finally driven out of Jerusalem, has been jealously guarded against the profanation which in Islamite eyes it would undergo if a Christian were to wander over its area, where Christ his Master so often trod; and, as instant death has always awaited the intruder who should be detected, few even of the most zealous topographists have cared to brave such a risk. In the year 1856, however, after the Crimean war, travellers were allowed to explore the Haram on payment of a pound a head. Since 1856 the enclosure has again been inaccessible to strangers, and before that year most of our trustworthy information respecting the interior of the buildings, the vaults, etc., was derived from the account of Mr. Catherwood, who succeeded in making plans and drawings of all the chief objects of interest under the following circumstances.

In the year 1833, during the rule of Mehemet Ali in Syria, he came to Jerusalem with a firman which named him engineer in the service of his highness. He was dressed as an Egyptian officer, and was accompanied by a brave and reckless Egyptian servant; and one day, notwithstanding the remonstrances of his friends, he walked into the Haram with an indifferent air, and taking care not to appear too curious, proceeded to examine it. As he was on the point of entering the great Mosque of Omar, he saw one of the dervishes who guard and show it off coming towards him to offer his services, in the hope of a handsome gratuity from the well-dressed stranger; but as the British interloper was not sufficiently skilled in the ceremonies to be gone through by a devout Islamite in a shrine of such sanctity, he turned away as if by accident, and left the enclosure without having attracted any notice. Emboldened by this success, he tried an extremely hazardous experiment the next day, for he took a camera lucida into the Haram with him, and sitting down began to make a drawing. This was a proceeding certain to attract the attention of the most indifferent, and almost to court their hostility, for the Moslem mind seems to have an innate suspicion of paper and pencil, and a marked repugnance to implements of such questionable orthodoxy. In such a case, what attracts notice at once rouses suspicion, and what excites suspicion instantaneously breeds danger of instant death.

Several Moslems looked doubtfully upon the artist, but passed on, deceived by his dress and the calm assurance with which he and his servant regarded them; but soon some bigots began to collect in groups at a distance, and grew excited in their talk. They approached, and then broke out into loud threats and curses; and surrounding the intruder, seemed to be screwing up their courage for a sudden rush upon him and his companion, which would have put a final and fatal stop to their adventures, but for an unexpected providential occurrence.

Suleiman, the Egyptian servant, in the middle of the mob, affected great indignation, returned threat for threat, and even struck some of the foremost with his whip, and knocked off the cap of a holy dervish; but as no satisfactory explanation of Mr. Catherwood's presence in the Haram could have been given, the tumult could only have ended at last in his being pulled to pieces by the infuriated Islamites, when an event occurred which converted in a moment the extremity of danger into the plenitude of success. The pacha, who governed Jerusalem for Mehemet Ali, appeared, with his suite, on the scene, and those of the assailants who had been struck by Suleiman's whip rushed up to him to demand the instant punishment of the infidel and his follower, who in that holy place horsewhipped true believers. Mr. Catherwood happened to be well acquainted with the pacha; and the latter, who was somewhat lax in matters of faith, supposing it altogether beyond the bounds of possibility that Mr. Catherwood would have ventured upon his undertaking without warrant from the sovereign himself, at once proceeded to pacify the indignation of the outraged believers. He told them that the great mosque was dilapidated, and that no doubt their master, Mehemet Ali, meant to repair it; and not finding a Moslem

THE TOMB OF ABSALOM.

who could make the requisite plans, must have sent a Christian for the purpose. He then threatened to inflict summary punishment on any one who dared for the future to interrupt Mehemet Ali's surveyor.

After this, all went on quietly, and for six weeks Mr. Catherwood examined every part of the Haram himself, and also introduced his companions, Messrs. Bonomi and Armadale, as necessary assistants.

At the expiration of six weeks, Ibrahim Pacha, the heir to Mehemet Ali's power and generalissimo of his forces, approached Jerusalem. Mr. Catherwood thought it wise to depart the day before Ibrahim entered the city, but his exploit caused rather a laughable mystification. Some English travellers of distinction arrived at the same time as Ibrahim Pacha, and applied to him for permission to visit the Haram. Ibrahim told them they might go if they liked, but he would not insure their safe return, and that he could not venture to outrage Moslem prejudices so far as to send an escort with them. They mentioned Mr. Catherwood's recent employment there: Ibrahim Pacha said the thing was impossible, but made further inquiries. He summoned the dervishes, and then the governor; and ere long the whole mistake was cleared up, arousing mingled sensations of astonishment, anger, and amusement among all the faithful who were present at the explanation.

The Haram, as watchfully guarded now by the Islamite against the entrance of the stranger as was the Temple by the Jew of yore, is by far the fairest spot in the holy city. It is the park or pleasure ground of Moslem Jerusalem. Over its spacious area are scattered many pleasing structures, small mosques, fountains covered by cupolas, rows of light graceful arches, open praying places, and small shrines crowned with domes erected over spots of peculiar sanctity, and along its western side run arcades and dwellings for the dervishes. Old trees, large and picturesque, olive, cypress, and plane, sometimes standing alone, sometimes grouped in small groves, give abundant shade; and there the faithful lounged and talked, or Moslem women sat and chattered, whilst their children sported around.

But the great ornament of this holy and beautiful enclosure, and of Jerusalem itself, is the world-famous Mosque of Omar, more correctly called the "Kubbet es-Sükhrah," or "The Dome of the Rock." Rising from the centre of a platform partly paved with marble, this elegant building, crowned by its light graceful dome, forms the most striking object in almost all views of the holy city. Its walls are inlaid with marble, and its windows brilliant with stained glass. Filling up most of the space beneath the dome, is an extraordinary relic: a huge mass of unhewn rock, of irregular shape and about sixty feet in its extreme length, rises five or six feet above the pavement of the mosque, and seventeen feet above the Haram level. Around this grey remnant of the limestone crown of Mount Moriah hover a host of traditions, Christian and Moslem. For near twelve hundred years the noble cupola of the khalif has sheltered the rough unsightly block which in Moslem eyes has a sanctity scarcely inferior to that of the Caabah at Mecca. Mohammed said, " The first of places is Jerusalem, and the first of rocks is the Sŭkhrah, and the rock Es-Sŭkhrah is one of the rocks of paradise." The mosque was built over it because it was supposed to mark the site of the Temple. David stood on it, and saw the angels descending by a golden ladder which rested on it; Solomon stood on it, sacrificing and offering the consecration prayer of his newly built temple. It was the place on which the ark rested, and towards which Israel prayed. On the rock is still shown the alleged footprint of the prophet, impressed at the moment when he mounted the famous ass Borak for his nocturnal journey to heaven. The rock bowed to the prophet in gratitude at the honour he had done to it by using it as a stepping stone; and on the opposite side the eyes of the faithful can distinguish the finger marks of some angels who helped it to perform this remarkable obeisance.

The Christians of the middle ages regarded the Sŭkhrah as the stone on which Jacob slept when he saw the vision of angels, and also as the spot where the avenging angel stood on Ornan's threshing-floor. Some also considered that it had supported the holy of holies of the Temple, and that it still contained hidden in itself the ark and other sacred things.

At the south-eastern side of the venerated rock is a chamber of irregular form, averaging seven feet high. This is called by Mohammedans " the Noble Cave," from their belief that in it Abraham, David, Solomon, and Jesus had successively prayed. In the centre of the rocky pavement is a circular slab of marble, which being struck returns a hollow sound, showing that there is a well or excavation of some kind beneath. This is called " the Well of the Spirits," some call it " the Gate of Hell, others " the Gate of Paradise." In the roof of the cave above this well is a cylindrical aperture, piercing the whole thickness of the rock above; and this is a fact of importance, as " the pierced rock " is connected with the identification of the Temple site.

The tomb of Absalom, of which an engraving is given, has been already fully described in the account of the monuments in the Valley of Jehoshaphat.

## XIX.
## JERUSALEM AND ITS SIEGES.

"Walk about Zion, go round about her, tell the towers thereof, mark ye well her bulwarks." From the day when Joab scaled the walls of the scoffing Jebusites, and won the stronghold of Zion for David, his uncle and king, the name of Jerusalem has always been suggestive of power and strength, and of defences all but impregnable. Her Temple in itself was a mighty fortress; and even when the besieging Roman had stormed and burned it, the citadel of Zion still defied the pagan host led by Titus. All was in vain: the face of the God of Jacob was turned away from its defenders.

From the peculiarity of her geographical position, Jerusalem must always have been greatly exposed to attack. She was the capital of a small though sturdy and wealthy state; but her hereditary foes, the Philistine and the Moabite, were close at hand on the east and west, whilst to the northward, Judah had much to fear from his brother Israel, and from Israel's occasional ally, the king of Damascus. But she had mightier foes than these, for she lay almost directly in the track along which the despots who swayed the rival empires of Egypt and Assyria alternately led their hosts against each other. The riches which adorned her shrines and were heaped up in her palaces, tempted every leader to invest her on his march; and over and over again do we read of additions being made to her walls and defences by every one of her monarchs who had Judah's honour at heart.

As long as Solomon filled Israel's throne, Jerusalem was safe from any hostile attempts of her warlike neighbours; but within four years after the accession of the foolish Rehoboam, it became known in Egypt that the custody of the vast wealth accumulated by Solomon had fallen into weak hands. Then "it came to pass that in the fifth year of king Rehoboam, Shishak king of Egypt came up against Jerusalem, because they had transgressed against the Lord," with an enormous host to seize the rich prize.

God, by the mouth of Shemaiah, pronounced judgment on the king and the princes of Judah, because they had forsaken him. Rehoboam capitulated at once; and the gold of the Temple, with the treasures of the king's house, and the golden shields hung up by Solomon in the house of the forest of Lebanon, were carried off into Egypt.

Incited by the report of this rich booty, which was handed down to him by tradition, Zerah, the king of Ethiopia, in the reign of Asa, invaded Judah with a countless host; but Judah's monarch was one of her most God-fearing kings, and to God he prayed in a strain which may well be imitated by rulers, by people, and by individuals on all occasions of danger or distress. "Lord, it is nothing with thee to help, whether with many, or with them that have no power: help us, O Lord our God; for we rest on thee, and in thy name we go against this multitude. O Lord, thou art our God; let not man prevail against thee." The Ethiopians, in answer to Asa's prayer, "were destroyed before the Lord and before his host;" but when, years after, the king of Israel came against Jerusalem, Asa sent the treasures of the Temple to purchase the help of the king of Syria; and because he trusted in man and not in God, the rest of his reign was troubled by wars.

In Jehoram's reign, Jerusalem was stormed by the Philistines and Arabs, and despoiled of her treasures. In the reign of Joash, the king of Syria laid siege to the holy city, but was induced to retire by payment of a ransom from the treasures of the Temple and palace. In Amaziah's reign, Jerusalem was taken and partly dismantled by Joash, king of Israel; but Uzziah repaired the walls, added towers, and otherwise strengthened the fortifications of the city; and his son, Jotham, continued these works, so that when Rezin of Damascus, and Pekah of Israel, besieged the city, it held out for a long time, and finally escaped capture.

The next famous siege was that by the Assyrians under Sennacherib, in Hezekiah's reign. When the news of the Assyrian invasion reached the good king, he repaired and added to the defences of his capital; and, as we have already mentioned, he stopped the springs and filled up the wells outside the city. For a time Hezekiah averted the scourge of war from Jerusalem by the payment of a ransom, and Sennacherib then marched southward; but the respite was not of long duration, for he sent his captains to summon the city to surrender. Hezekiah "made darts and shields in abundance," but he had a better ground for reliance than even his strong walls and his numerous weapons; and he told his people, "Be strong and courageous; be not afraid nor dismayed for the king of Assyria, nor for all the multitude that is with him: for there be more with us than with him. With him is an arm of flesh; but with us is the Lord our God to help us, and to fight our battles. And the people rested themselves upon the words of Hezekiah king of Judah." King

THE GATE OF THE COLUMN, COMMONLY CALLED THE DAMASCUS GATE.

and people alike put their whole trust in Jehovah, and " the Lord saved Hezekiah and the inhabitants of Jerusalem from the hand of Sennacherib, the king of Assyria, who had railed against the Holy One of Israel in boasting and in blasphemy; for ere an arrow had been shot against the holy city, an angel smote a hundred and eighty-five thousand men of war in the besieging camp, and the arrogant monarch fled away " with shame of face to his own land," there to die by the hands of his own sons.

" The virgin daughter of Zion," during Hezekiah's life-time, laughed her assailants to scorn; but in his wicked son's reign, she was for a time a captive, and her king was carried to Babylon. On his restoration, we read that he repaired the old walls and built a fresh one. After Josiah's reign, Pharaoh Necho, king of Egypt, imprisoned his successor, Jehoahaz, and heavily taxed Jerusalem. Nebuchadnezzar, king of Babylon, then took Jerusalem, carried her king Jehoiachin captive, and in his stead appointed Zedekiah as king and tributary; but he rebelled against his master, who at once laid siege to the city. So strong were its defences, that though Nebuchadnezzar himself directed the attack, and lofty mounds were raised against it, and battering rams constantly beat against the walls, yet a year and a half passed before it fell. A breach had been made in the wall; and through it, in the dead of night, the generals of the besieging army entered with their forces, slaughtered the inhabitants, and sacked the city, which was then dismantled and burned. The Jews who had escaped the sword were carried to Babylon, a remnant of Judah's thickly peopled land.

Nabopolassar, a Babylonian by birth, and general of the Assyrian army, rebelled against his effeminate master, usurped the monarchy of Babylon, and at length, with the help of the king of the Medes, destroyed great Nineveh, and made Babylon the sole capital of his empire. His son, Nebuchadnezzar, worked out to the very letter all that God's prophets had long before foretold.

At length the weary captivity ended, and Judah's children no longer wept by the waters of Babylon. Then the Temple was rebuilt, and, under the direction of Nehemiah, a new wall and new gates were raised around the ruined city; priests, nobles, and people, with but one recorded exception, uniting to do the work of their Lord.

Long after this, Ptolemy Soter took Jerusalem, partly by treachery, and partly because, when he had effected an entrance, the Jews would offer no resistance, as the attack took place on the sabbath day. They gave themselves up, without a struggle, to slaughter; and Ptolemy thus made himself complete master of the city, and carried away many of its inhabitants to Egypt. After this the high priest, Simon the Just, "fortified the Temple, and built the high fortress of the wall about it, and fortified the city against besiegers."

Jerusalem was nevertheless taken and retaken by the sovereigns of Syria and Egypt, and suffered also from internal feuds. The tyrant Antiochus Epiphanes, king of Syria, first plundered the Temple and city, and carried away many captives, and afterwards sent an army which, on the sabbath, stormed Jerusalem and made a great slaughter. The city was plundered and burned, and much of its wall destroyed; but Zion was garrisoned and more strongly fortified than ever. The site of the Temple was dedicated to the Olympian Jupiter; swine were sacrificed on God's altar, and the broth from boiled pigs' flesh was sprinkled about to defile the Temple and its courts. It was not the will of God, however, that Jerusalem should perish utterly, or that his worship there should yet cease.

Modern Jerusalem has five open gates. The Hebron or Jaffa Gate on the west; the "Gate of the prophet David" or "the Zion Gate," and a small gate but little used, and called the "Gate of the Western Africans," or the "Dung Gate," on the south. The "Gate of St. Stephen," also called the "Gate of the Tribes," or the "Gate of the Lady Mary," on the east; and the "Báb el Amúd," the "Gate of the Column," or the "Damascus Gate," on the north. The last is the most ornamental, and is a handsome specimen of Saracenic architecture. From it runs the great road northward to Damascus. Above the city wall on the right are seen the domes and tower of the church of the Holy Sepulchre, and also the square mass of the tower of David. At the base of the gateway towers are some ancient stones, and within the towers are some old Jewish chambers, whose walls are entirely constructed of stones similar in workmanship to those at the corners of the Temple area. From the chamber in the eastern tower, a winding staircase leads to the top of the wall, and the masonry of its sides is of a similar character to that below. It is probable that the towers of the Damascus Gate are built upon the remains of the guardhouses of an ancient gate of Jewish date.

The north-eastern quarter of the city is but thinly peopled. Most of the space within the wall is covered with ruins and rubbish, or occupied by gardens and patches of wheat. The whole of the north-east corner of the city is one continuous corn-field. There is a tower with a walled-up gateway between the Damascus Gate and the north-eastern angle of the city wall. The natives call it the "Gate of Flowers," but by Europeans it is known as the Gate of Herod. Another gate has long been walled up. This is the famous "Golden Gate" in the eastern wall of the Haram, concerning whose date there has been much controversy.

## XX.
## THE HOLY SEPULCHRE.

When Titus laid siege to Jerusalem, the city was defended by a triple wall, except where the nature of the ground made a single rampart impregnable. These walls were raised at different periods. The first wall, or wall of Zion, was built or strengthened by David, Solomon, and their successors. It started from the north-western corner of Zion, at the point where Herod built the tower of Hippicus, and ran eastward to the Temple. Southward, it followed the western brow of Zion to the gate of the Essenes, whose site is unknown, and thence it ran along the southern crest of the hill and across the Tyropœon, till it joined the Temple colonnade at Ophel.

Concerning the course of the second wall, many a learned controversy and many a keen dispute has arisen, for it involves a very important matter, namely, the trustworthiness of ecclesiastical tradition. This second wall inclosed the quarter of Akra, encircled only the northern quarter of the city, and terminated at Antonia. Now this wall existed in our Saviour's time; and if it ran so far to the northward that the old foundations of bevelled stones in the city wall near the Latin convent, and the remains of which we have spoken at the Damascus Gate, formed part of it, then the reputed "Holy Sepulchre" can have no claim whatever to the title, though ecclesiastical tradition for more than fifteen centuries has pointed out the cave enshrined in the splendid structure Constantine first founded as the real tomb in which our Lord was laid.

The third wall, or wall of Bezetha, was not built till after our Lord's death, and it also inclosed a great space to the northward. It started from Hippicus, and passing opposite the monument of Helena, joined the old wall at the valley of the Kidron.

The present wall of Jerusalem was built by Sultan Sulieman in A.D. 1542, and appears to occupy very nearly the same site as the wall of the middle ages, which followed in a great measure the course of that built by Hadrian.

Among all the mummeries which are annually performed by the monks and their abettors in Jerusalem, there is one enacted in the church of the Holy Sepulchre upon Easter eve which exceeds all others in impiety. Year after year, on that day, the house of God is profaned by the blasphemous imposture which is called "The Miracle of the Holy Fire." Early on that morning the church is filled with a dense throng of Greek Christians, except where a circular lane surrounding the chapel of the Holy Sepulchre, and a part of the crowd around it, is kept open by two ranks of Turkish soldiers. Towards noon the pilgrims gradually grow violently excited, and groups of them break into this ring, and rush frantically round and round the tomb, dancing, jumping on each other's shoulders, and performing other uncouth gambols, whilst all the time they clap their hands and utter wild cries and howls. Suddenly the course is cleared, and a gorgeous procession, with embroidered banners borne aloft, thrice marches round the ring. A small band of ecclesiastics surrounding "the bishop of the fire," force their way to the chapel door, which admits the bishop and is closed after his entry. In the outer wall of the chapel is a hole, at which stands a priest, and from the aperture to the church wall a narrow lane is made through the dense crowd. The worshippers are now wound up to the highest pitch of fervour, when suddenly a bright flame appears in the hole. The priest lights his torch, and then from all directions there is a rush to reach the fire, and the illumination spreads over the church till it is a-blaze with thousands of lighted torches and tapers. Then there is a rush towards the door to escape the heat and smoke; and the fanatics hurry from house to house, carrying the fire through Jerusalem.

Now the abomination of this performance consists in its being asserted by the clergy, and firmly believed by the deluded laity, that the Holy Spirit descends in fire upon the sacred tomb. And when the flame has blazed out, the bishop of the fire, who of course had kindled it from the inside, is borne out on the shoulders of the people in a pretended faint, so that it may appear that he is overcome by the glory of the Almighty, in whose immediate presence he has just been.

Anciently, all the Christian churches participated in the ceremony; but when the Latins were expelled from the church by the Greeks, and could no longer share in the profits of the exhibition, they denounced it as a fraud. The Armenians afterwards followed their example. To the Greek community, this monkish fraud is the one great attraction in the Holy City, which draws them away in pilgrimage from their distant homes.

ENTRANCE TO THE CHURCH OF THE HOLY SEPULCHRE.

## XXI.

## THE MOUNT OF OLIVES.

OF the mountains which encompass Jerusalem, the Mount of Olives is both the most prominent and the most interesting. Olivet is not so much a single mount as a ridge with three rounded summits of about equal elevation, and it is the central hill to which the honoured name is more especially applied. The range runs north and south, and is divided from Jerusalem only by the narrow Valley of Jehoshaphat.

A small village crowns the summit of the central hill, and its mosque and minaret are conspicuous objects from most points in and near Jerusalem. Its elevation above the sea is stated to be 2,556 Paris feet. Aged olive trees are grouped about it, and are somewhat scantily sprinkled upon the mountain's western face. Perhaps the thicker groves and more luxuriant gardens of the olden time may have shown richer and fresher in the glaring midday hour; but when the sinking sun shines in rosy hues, or blazes in golden glory upon the sacred mount, tinging with lovely colour the pearly grey of the limestone rock and terrace walls, and warming the delicate tones of the fresh green corn which streaks in narrow bands the broken hill-side; when its graceful undulating outline glows radiant against the cool eastern sky, and all the gentle heavings of its flanks are softly marked and defined by violet shades—at that fleeting hour, Olivet is fairer than of yore.

Olivet is full of associations that are grateful to the Christian; and it is with a loving interest that his ear and heart respond to the sound of its name. It was the favourite haunt of Him who, while in his mingled nature of God and man he was borne down by the load of the world's iniquities, yet as a man had human feelings, but without sin. Hither, for quiet after the turmoil of the crowd, for the rest needed after hard labour in his Father's work, for calm converse with his chosen followers, and for secret communion with his Father, he habitually resorted. He loved the Mount and its precincts, and sought in its cool shades and glorious prospects a human solace. "In the day time he was teaching in the Temple, and at night he went out and abode in the mount that is called the Mount of Olives." It was as he sat upon the Mount of Olives that his disciples came to him privately, for the explanation of his mysterious predictions respecting the destruction of the great building of the Temple, of the signs of his coming, and of the end of the world. Here, while as man he rested in the shade of the fair groves, he unfolded to them, as the Christ, all his dark sayings, and fully enlightened their understanding. Here, to them, and to all who would believe in his mission of redemption, he gave many a clue to guide them in the troublous days to come, and many a warning to prevent their being led astray by false Christs and false prophets. Here, too, he spoke a prophecy whose full accomplishment each revolving year steadily and surely brings nearer and nearer, that before the end "the gospel must first be published in all nations;" and here he spoke the words of encouragement—" Heaven and earth shall pass away, but my words shall not pass away;" and of advice—" And what I say unto you, I say unto all, Watch."

It was in moments of quiet seclusion that the Redeemer spoke thus; but these scenes were to resound with the acclamations of a host, whose loud hosannas proclaimed that he who meekly rode upon the foal of an ass, and whom they escorted in triumph, was in very truth the King who came in the name of the Lord. Over the shoulder of Olivet the vast throng swept; and as the glorious prospect of the city burst upon their sight, the man Jesus, touched by human sympathy for the human sufferings his Divinity foreknew, wept over the doomed city that would not know the truth.

The triumph was over, the agony had been undergone, the rent veil of the Temple had testified that sin's penalty was paid, and that the new dispensation had begun; the Pharisees' broken seals, and Joseph of Arimathea's open sepulchre, told of the crowning victory over Satan and the grave; and then for the last time, over the Mount of Olives, by the oft-travelled road towards Bethany, the risen Christ led his disciples forth. Then, on the slopes of Olivet, when Jerusalem was lost to sight, he raised his hands and blessed his followers: thence he was taken from them up to heaven; and as the intervening cloud hid him from their bodily eyes, angels appeared and spoke to them; and with weary hearts they turned from sacred Olivet to begin their apostolic mission and win the martyr's crown.

Such are the associations which link the Mount of Olives with our Lord's sojourn upon earth; and here we have no room for doubt that often and often his presence sanctified its rocks, and slopes, and shades. We cannot wonder, therefore, that the soil of this real abiding place of the Saviour has been encrusted with traditions, many of which date from a very early epoch.

THE SUMMIT OF THE MOUNT OF OLIVES.

## XXII.

## VIEW FROM OLIVET.

ECCLESIASTICAL tradition tells us that our Lord ascended to heaven from the *summit* of the Mount of Olives, and this is one of the earliest Christian traditions concerning the sacred sites within or around the Holy City; but ecclesiastical tradition, unless supported by other authority, scriptural or historical, is by itself of questionable value, and when it is opposed to trustworthy evidence, is absolutely worthless. Now, in the present instance tradition is directly at variance with the plain letter of Scripture. We read that Jesus led his disciples " out as far as to Bethany; and he lifted up his hands, and blessed them; and it came to pass, while he blessed them, he was parted from them and carried up into heaven." This statement is quite explicit; but we have the additional fact that, after the ascension, the disciples returned " unto Jerusalem from the mount called Olivet, which is from Jerusalem a sabbath day's journey." And, to connect the two places, we read in another passage—" And when they came nigh to Jerusalem, unto Bethphage and Bethany, *at the Mount* of Olives;" so that Bethany is plainly treated as part of the Mount of Olives. The summit of the Mount, according to the best authorities, is much within a sabbath day's journey, and therefore, unless we place more value upon a vague tradition than upon the clear word of Scripture, we must take it for granted that our Lord ascended from some secluded spot in the immediate vicinity of favoured Bethany.

Before the days of the Empress Helena, Eusebius relates that multitudes of Christians paid their adorations on the summit of the Mount of Olives, whence Jesus ascended into heaven. The empress built a church over the site, but that has long since disappeared. Now, the legendary site is marked by a modern octagonal chapel, in a paved court belonging to a mosque, in the custody of a dervish.

Ascending the minaret, the most comprehensive view of all the country about Jerusalem is obtained; and at a sheikh's tomb, the view to the eastward is better seen than from the minaret. The foreground is cultivated with plots of corn between the outcroppings of the limestone rock, but the wild rugged tract upon which we look down seems all barren and arid. Bare hills, seamed by deep ravines, stretch in ceaseless undulations to a broad sheet of water far away, that glares in the sunlight. Closing the view beyond the distant waters, a lofty wall of rugged mountain falls precipitously to the water's eastern brink; and from its northern shore a plain, divided by a stream of whose windings we catch an occasional glimpse, spreads away to the northward.

This is a strangely interesting view, for that stream is the Jordan. In that plain stood Jericho. That glistening water is the Dead Sea. Those distant mountains were the strongholds of Moab and Ammon, and the nearer hills belonged to the wilderness of Judah. Whilst all that we gaze on from Olivet's brow towards the sunrising is suggestive of sterility and death, the prospect towards the setting sun speaks of life and hope. True it is that glory is gone and beauty faded; but though the crown has been dashed from her brow, yet amid Zion's ruins a people still dwells, and the voice of childhood rings through the air, whilst the hills and vales around her reward with a moderate yield the labourer's toil. From this brow we look down upon the terraced roofs of the city, can map out its plan, and identify all its leading features.

Among the many fabulous "Holy Places" upon Olivet are a chapel where Jesus is reported to have taught his disciples the Lord's Prayer; the spot where the angel stood who gave the Virgin three days' warning before her death; some vaults where the apostles composed the Creed; the cell in which the fair and frail Pelagia of Antioch passed many a year in penitence and penance; the spot where a tower, called "Viri Galilei," was built on the place where the two angels appeared to the disciples after our Lord's ascension; the point where Jesus wept over the city; and many others of no greater authenticity.

We have dwelt on the associations of Olivet only as connected with the earthly sojourn of the Messiah; but it bore a part in the history of his ancestor David on a memorable occasion. Absalom had rebelled against his father; "the conspiracy was strong, for the people increased continually with Absalom;" and David and his household fled from Jerusalem. The king passed over the Brook Kidron, and sent back the ark of God to its sanctuary in the Temple: and then "David went up by the ascent of Mount Olivet, and wept as he went up, and had his head covered, and he went barefoot; and all the people that was with him covered every man his head; and they went up, weeping as they went up."

THE DEAD SEA AND THE MOUNTAINS OF MOAB FROM THE MOUNT OF OLIVES.

## XXIII.

## "THE TOWN OF MARY AND HER SISTER MARTHA."

BETHANY has no Old Testament history. The Gospel story, and that alone, has made its name a household word throughout Christendom. Every incident in its history is closely connected with Christ, with his private life, with his domestic affections, with his miracles, his preaching, and with that short triumphal progress which had been foretold for so many centuries. This was the village in which Jesus "lodged" during the last few days of his life on earth. "Jesus loved Martha, and her sister, and Lazarus;" and Bethany was "the town of Mary and her sister Martha." Here, with a mortal sorrow, he wept with grieving relatives over his dead friend; and here by his Divine power he restored that lost friend to life and sisterly love. Here was the house of Simon the leper, where Mary anointed Christ as he sat at meat, with the precious ointment of spikenard, which good work has, in fulfilment of the prophecy Christ then spoke, been told as a memorial of her wherever the gospel has been preached; here, too, Martha was tenderly reproved for her too great earnestness about worldly matters, to the exclusion of things spiritual; and, last of all, it was among the uplands that overhang the village that his disciples talked with their Master for the last time, and when he was gone from them heard the words, "This same Jesus, which is taken up from you into heaven, shall so come in like manner as ye have seen him go into heaven."

There is no doubt whatever about the site of Bethany; and in its modern name, El'Azariyeh, a remembrance of Lazarus is preserved. The name of "Bethany" has disappeared for ages, and very suitable is its changed appellation; for almost all the interest it possesses is inseparably linked with the family whom Jesus loved, and with the great miracle he wrought on their behalf.

Three paths lead to the village from Jerusalem, and every one of these must often have been trodden by our Lord and his disciples. Two lead over the summit of the Mount of Olives; the third, which is the main road to Jericho, passes round the southern shoulder of the hill. It was probably by this latter road that Jesus passed in triumph on the ass's colt; and the view of Jerusalem over which he wept must have been almost the same as that from the Mount of

Offence which has been described. A rocky ridge hides Bethany from the top of the Mount of Olives, for it is situated in a wooded hollow on the eastern slope of the Mount. The village stands on a rocky knoll, and is wretched and ruinous enough. The houses are built of old materials, among which are bevelled stones which must have stood in the house walls of the town of Mary in Mary's day. At that time, when the terraces were kept in order, the gardens rich in palm and fruit trees, and the hills green with corn, Bethany, "the house of dates," must have been a sweet secluded spot, whose freshness and tranquillity must have contrasted delightfully with the glare and turmoil of the thronged city; and even now, though cultivation is much neglected by the lazy and unthrifty peasants who tenant it, yet surrounded as it is by groups of olives, pomegranates, almond and fig trees, and by sloping hills and broken rocks, it retains much that is cheerful and picturesque.

No palms now wave their feathery branches over Bethany and her gardens. The prominent feature is a massive block of ancient masonry which towers above her houses, and, built of bevelled stones and standing on a scarped rock, more resembles, from its strength and situation, a fort than a private residence. This is the traditional house of Mary and Martha; but satisfactory evidence of its authenticity is wanting. At the same time there is no conclusive evidence to rebut the assumption. The house of Simon the leper is also pointed out; and beneath a building marked in our sketch by a small minaret is the so-called tomb of Lazarus. Passing through a low entrance and down a long flight of worn steps into a rock-hewn chamber, a few more steps lead down to a smaller vault, in which the corpse of Lazarus is said to have lain, and whence at the Almighty's word the dead came forth, bound hand and foot with grave clothes. It is scarcely probable that the tomb was in the middle of the town; but we do not require these sites to be authenticated to convince us that we are on holy ground. The presence of Christ pervades Bethany and its neighbourhood. We know that the houses of the village received our Lord, and that every path about it was habitually trodden by the Saviour's feet; that the last undisturbed moments of his life were passed there; that there he raised the dead; and that, when he had offered up the all-sufficient sacrifice of himself, his last walk in bodily form upon earth hallowed the road that led thither; and finally, that from some spot in that sequestered vale, in sight of the dwelling places he had loved, he ascended to his Father in heaven. Bethany has no other history than this. Could we wish for fuller annals? Of Bethphage, its sister village, no trace exists.

BETHANY.

## XXIV.
## JERUSALEM AND ITS INHABITANTS.

"How doth the city sit solitary that was full of people! How is she become as a widow! She that was great among the nations, and princess among the provinces, how is she become tributary! She weepeth sore in the night, and her tears are on her cheeks. .... Judah is gone into captivity; .... she dwelleth among the heathen, she findeth no rest; .... and from the daughter of Zion all her beauty is departed." "How hath the Lord covered the daughter of Zion with a cloud in his anger, and cast down from heaven unto the earth the beauty of Israel, and remembered not his footstool in the day of his anger! The Lord hath swallowed up all the habitations of Jacob, and hath not pitied; he hath thrown down in his wrath the strongholds of the daughter of Judah." .... "The Lord hath cast off his altar; he hath abhorred his sanctuary; he hath given up into the hand of the enemy the walls of her palaces. All that pass by clap their hands at them, they hiss and wag their head at the daughter of Jerusalem, saying, Is this the city that men call the perfection of beauty, the joy of the whole earth?"

From the slopes of Olivet, from the brow of the Mount of Offence, from the summit of Scopus, a hasty glance is quite sufficient to show us that these stern predictions have had their complete and literal accomplishment, and that "the Lord hath done that which he had devised: he hath fulfilled his word." Shrunken and forlorn, the mere shadow of her former self, the fallen Jerusalem now crouches upon the splendid site which Judah's monarchs once made so glorious. The enemy has swept from Zion the walls of her palaces, the monuments of her kings; and fields of grain or gardens of herbs flourish upon their site. There is not a hut upon Ophel, or a hovel in that great northern suburb which Agrippa enclosed. The site of the Xystus, and the valley of the Tyropœon are encumbered with rubbish and filth, and within the contracted limits of the modern town is many a desolate tract covered with ruin or sown with corn. There is life within her walls; but how dwindled is her population! There is no stir in her streets, which were once so "full of people," and they seem almost deserted to the stranger's eye. Her present inhabitants are approximately estimated at about thirteen thousand.

What they were in the days of her glory we cannot tell, for we are altogether without data on the subject. At the time of the siege by Titus, the city was crowded with strangers, who had come up to the Feast of the Passover; and, according to Josephus, it would appear that there were 1,200,000 people within the walls. Tacitus gives just half the number, and many believe that in his account the numbers of the besieged are overstated. "The precious sons of Zion comparable to fine gold, how are they esteemed as earthen pitchers, the work of the hands of the potter!" Nearly half of the inhabitants of Jerusalem are Jews, but they are strangers and paupers where stood their ancient palaces and homes. Wretched and squalid, idle and dependent, they subsist almost entirely on contributions from Europe.

Leaving Jerusalem by the Jaffa Gate, and turning southward across the plain of Rephaim, just before mounting the hill to the convent of Mar Elias, there is in the very middle of the path a well to which tradition has appended a pretty legend, reminding the traveller that the road he is following leads to Bethlehem, and is full of recollections of the birth of Jesus. The wise men from the East had come to Herod in Jerusalem to inquire where they might find the new-born King of the Jews, and thence pursued their route to Bethlehem along this very road. It was night, and they were uncertain as to their further course; when, as they stooped over the well's brink to draw water, they suddenly saw the heavenly messenger that had led them from their own land, brightly mirrored in the still water below. They looked up, and saw it glistening over head, and followed it till it rested above the manger in which Jesus lay.

Rachel's tomb, the illustration on the opposite page, is soon reached. There is nothing imposing in the building which bears Rachel's name; but that it covers her dust there seems to be no doubt whatever. The Jew, the Moslem, and the Christian, honour it alike, and agree in their traditions respecting it. Hard by the spot marked by this simple monument, Jacob's tents were pitched, and around it his flocks pastured during that anxious time of heart-wearing suspense whilst "Rachel travailed and had hard labour;" and on its very site, when the worst was known, and Rachel was dead, the mourning patriarch reared a pillar over the grave in which he laid her. That pillar, Moses tells us, was standing when Jacob's posterity were restored to the land in which their ancestor had sojourned; and Samuel speaks of "Rachel's sepulchre in the border of Benjamin." Josephus alludes to it as "over against Ephrath" (Bethlehem), which describes its situation exactly. The Jews have recently succeeded in purchasing from the Moslems the shrine so dear to them, and around the grave of their mother their tombs are scattered.

RACHEL'S TOMB.

## XXV.

## "BETHLEHEM AND THE LAND OF JUDAH."

RACHEL was the wife of Jacob's affection. He had loved her, had wooed her, and had won her from her father by hard and valuable service. When the time came in which he was to receive his reward, he was defrauded by Laban, and he found that he had unconsciously become the husband of Rachel's plain sister Leah. We cannot wonder that Leah found but little love in her married life; but God, who looks upon mortal affairs with other eyes than those of mortals, blessed the neglected wife more than the loved sister she had supplanted. He blessed her with many more children; he blessed her with a longer life; and on her and not upon Rachel did he bestow the dignity of being the ancestress of Christ. Judah was son of Leah, David sprang from Judah, and Bethlehem formed part of Judah's heritage.

The sketch engraved in this chapter is taken from a field on the terraced hillside on the left of the road before entering Bethlehem. The town stands upon a limestone ridge, and seems never to have been a place of importance from its size or strength, though it is one of the most ancient towns in Palestine, and was fortified by Rehoboam. It has never played a part in secular history; but even before the birth of the Redeemer its houses and its inhabitants were famous, and to us the interest it excites is second only to that which Jerusalem arouses. It was the city of Christ's ancestry in the flesh. From thence Elimelech and his wife Naomi went forth to the land of Moab; and thither, when her husband's sons were dead, and the Almighty had dealt very bitterly with her, Naomi returned, and her daughter-in-law Ruth was with her. "And they came to Bethlehem in the beginning of barley harvest." Little thought Ruth of the high destiny that was in store for her when she clung in true affection to poor and aged Naomi, and deserted her land, her people, and their worship, for the stranger homes of Judah and the service of the Lord of hosts.

Every reader knows the simple tale of how she became the rich man's wife; but further and greater honour was in store for her, and she bore a son, through whom she, the daughter of the stranger and idolater, became the great-grandmother of King David, and the ancestress of the Messiah. At Bethlehem, as we study this page of the domestic history of the place, and these undoubted records of the manners and customs of its inhabitants in that old time, we can almost realize the scenes described. Our view is bounded by Ruth's native mountains, the rugged land of Moab, beyond Jordan: around us are the homes of Bethlehem, and at our feet are spread the fields in which she gleaned.

Time passes on; Naomi and Ruth and Obed are safe with Israel's God, and Jesse dwells in Bethlehem. Then, whilst upon those neighbouring hills David was tending sheep, Samuel came to Bethlehem, sanctified Jesse and his seven elder sons preparatory to offering sacrifice, and, as they passed before him one by one, announced that the Lord refused them, for he looked not upon the outward appearance, but on the heart. David was sent for, was chosen by the Lord, was anointed by Samuel, "and the Spirit of the Lord came upon David from that day forward." David's peaceful occupation ends, and he is soon lost to Bethlehem's pastures. The conqueror of Goliath, the favourite, and the son-in-law of Saul, sees little of his old haunts till the monarch's frenzied jealousy drives him to seek shelter as a fugitive in the wilderness of Judah. At one period of his troubled career the Philistines had taken and garrisoned Bethlehem; and David, in the thirsty wilderness, thought of his boyhood's home, and longed for water from the well of Bethlehem, from which he was wont to drink in boyhood and youth. So great was the power which he had acquired over the hearts of his companions, that without his request, or even his knowledge, three of his most distinguished followers broke through the Philistines' guards and perilled their lives to gratify his wish. In many ways this incident gives us an insight into David's character, both in his influence over others and his mastery of himself. He thought it wrong that men's lives should be jeopardized for the supply of his bodily wants, and he poured out the water of Bethlehem's well in libation to the Lord. Within a few minutes' walk of the modern town is a deep, wide cistern hewn in the rock. It has two or three openings, and is very ancient. It bears David's name, and may probably be the very one whose water the three mighty men bore away in evidence of their enthusiastic devotion to their leader. The pretty tale of early agricultural life contained in the book of Ruth gives a pleasant interest to Bethlehem and its corn-fields. As the birthplace of David, too, as the scene of his consecration by Samuel to Israel's throne, it claims a visit from the wandering stranger; but these associations with the old dispensation, noteworthy as they are, are altogether eclipsed by that one momentous occurrence which inspired the first paragraph of the covenant of grace.

In Bethlehem a virgin's child was born. The child lay humbly in a manger, but the glory of the Lord blazed through the midnight gloom. The messenger

of the Lord proclaimed the good tidings of salvation, joy, and peace; and in triumphal choir the Lord's host burst forth in strains of praise to God for his free love toward men. Over Bethlehem, until the eastern sages worshipped the new-born child, hung the star that had miraculously led them from their distant homes. Then when their faith saw a king in the young babe so meanly lodged, and they laid regal gifts at his feet, the bright messenger's mission ended and it vanished. In Bethlehem the wise men heard prophetic warning in their dreams, and meekly obeyed God's message thus conveyed. In Bethlehem, in the still night, Joseph, too, dreamt a dream, and under night's sheltering shades fled from David's city with his virgin wife and her royal child for safety to the Nile. From Bethlehem's mothers a long, loud wail of anguish rose when their innocent babes perished because the tyrant foolishly thought that by his savage mandate he could bring the sure word of God's prophecy to nought.

The sky, the hills, the vales, the rocks of Bethlehem saw these things come to pass. They heard the heavenly song, and shone in the divine refulgence of that holy midnight hour; and they are better witnesses to us of the all-important events of which Bethlehem was the scene than the cumbrous structures with which man has hidden the place which saw the Saviour's birth. They have been for ever consecrated by the advent of the Redeemer on that night. Bethlehem in the land of Judah is in very truth not the least among the princes of Judah. *There* dawned the light which illumines and benefits man while time is; and when time is no longer, guides him to a blessed eternity. The doctrine of Christ was the groundwork of civilization here, and the sacrifice of Christ the gateway to everlasting happiness hereafter. There is but one faith now in Bethlehem, and that is the faith of Him who was laid an infant in Bethlehem's manger; but alas! Christianity there is little more than nominal—rather a political than a religious distinction. The inhabitants now number about three thousand. They are peasants, and cultivate the fields and terraced gardens around, and some of them also carve crosses, rosaries, etc., for sale to the pilgrims. Before 1834 there was a moslem quarter in the town; but when the peasants revolted against Egyptian rule, it was destroyed by Ibrahim Pacha, and all the Mohammedans expelled. The Christians were disarmed, for they were a turbulent set, prone to revolt; but on this particular occasion they were supposed by the stern pacha to be less guilty than their moslem fellow citizens, with whom they had ever been at deadly feud. The mode in which the disarmament was carried out was altogether original, and to our European notions, intensely oriental. The Bethlehemites, and the people of other villages disarmed, were not called upon to give up all the arms they possessed, for in this case some might be held back, and at any rate it would be a work of trouble to find out whether all were given up or not; but they were required to surrender a specified number of weapons whether they possessed that quantity or not. The number was always made large enough to cover the whole of the arms which it was suspected might be in the hands of the peasants, and something more. The result of this rule was, that many of the poorer people had to search for and purchase arms at a ruinous price, to avoid being immured in prison or being taken for soldiers; whilst the richer classes bought worthless weapons and gave them up to the authorities, still keeping their own more valuable ones.

While the soldiers were carrying out this process in Bethlehem, and many of its inhabitants were in prison and all were in fear and distress, the English consul at Damascus, who was staying at Jerusalem, rode out to visit Solomon's Pools in company with one of the English missionaries. As he approached Bethlehem on his return, the people flocked out to meet him, and implore the help of England in their trouble; and then all at once they stripped off their outer garments and spread them in the way before the horse's feet of him whose power they thought might avail for their aid. The consul was affected to tears, but he was unable to interfere between the grim pacha and those who were for the time his subjects. The incident affords us an additional illustration of the truthfulness to nature of the events commemorated in Scripture, and of the permanence of manners of every kind in the unchanging East.

## XXVI.

## THE CONVENTS IN THE LAND OF JUDAH.

RIDING through Bethlehem, we soon come to the vast convent and church of the Nativity. There are many primitive legends, which invest the fields and rocks round Bethlehem with attractions for the votaries of superstition. The place where the shepherds watched their flocks on the night of the Redeemer's birth is pointed out, and so is the village in which they dwelt. Over the Grotto of the Nativity at Bethlehem, a splendid basilica was erected by the Empress Helena about 327—the oldest Christian edifice in the world. It is about 120 feet long and 110 feet broad, and is divided into a central nave and four side aisles, by rows of Corinthian columns of marble, which may not improbably have previously belonged to the porches of the Temple at Jerusalem. A wall is built across the end of this nave, to separate it from the choir. It is neglected, and falling into ruin; the pavement is broken, the mosaics which once adorned its walls have almost disappeared, and the roof is much out of repair. It is invested by noisy swarms of dealers in rosaries, crosses, carvings, etc., in olive wood, stones of olives, and mother of pearl from the Red Sea, who turn the house of prayer into a den of thieves.

The great object of attraction is beneath the choir, of which half belongs to the Greeks and half to the Armenians, whilst the Latins have a church branching off from its northern side. All three sects have staircases and passages to the sacred grottoes underground. "The Altar of the Innocents" is said to mark the spot where twenty thousand of the children slain by Herod's order were buried. An iron door leads to the chapel of the Nativity, a low vault hewn in the rock. In the pavement of a small semicircular recess is a marble slab, in which is a silver star, with the words, "Here Jesus Christ was born of the Virgin Mary," inscribed round it in Latin. Sixteen silver lamps suspended round the star are constantly kept burning. The whole vault is overlaid with marble and paintings, and gold and silver, silk and embroidery; and there is nothing whatever in this gorgeous crypt that speaks to our hearts of the new-born Christ and Bethlehem's stable, except the few thrilling words of the simple inscription quoted above.

In St. Matthew's Gospel we are told that when the star which led the wise men of the East had shown them the place where the young child was, they came into "*the house*," and saw the young child with Mary his mother; and in the absence of any satisfactory explanation, it seems difficult to believe that this subterranean vault would be designated as a house by the inspired evangelist. We can, however, feel sure that "Beit Lahm," "The House of Flesh," is identical with Bethlehem, "The House of Bread," where Christ was born. Very near this spot, that wonderful mystery was brought about: more cannot be said.

Three convents, belonging to the Greeks, Latins, and Armenians respectively, join the church of the Nativity, and form altogether an enormous pile, which more resembles a fortress than an ecclesiastical edifice.

A ride through ravines and over bare plateaus for nearly three hours, reaches the extraordinary convent of Mar Saba. The convent is a strange construction, placed in a most singular position. The gorge of the Kidron at this point is gloomy and savage beyond description. Ragged precipices on each side fall into its stony bed; and on the face of the western cliff, where a small side ravine breaks the wall of rock and falls abruptly into the torrent, hangs the religious edifice which bears St. Saba's name. Every narrow ledge, every rugged projection, has been turned to account to afford a communication or support a buttress; but still the whole building looks as if it were on the point of slipping from its strange perch and tumbling into the chasm below. In its construction advantage has been taken of natural caves in the face of the cliff, and of artificial excavations scooped out by the labour of the earlier anchorites. In front of these, other cells have been built wherever a shelf of rock could be found; and long intricate narrow galleries winding over the precipice, and interminable flights of stairs, afford roundabout communications from one group of cells to another. The church occupies the point of the rock, and is upheld by enormous buttresses which spring from the depths of the abyss. It forms a prominent feature in the sketch given in this chapter. Usually, travellers bring credentials from Jerusalem, and on these being read, the number of persons specified are admitted, provided they are of the nobler sex, for no female foot may cross the threshold. Ladies may encamp outside and protect themselves as best they may against storms and robbers; or they may occupy one of two lofty watch towers which stand outside the walls, and which are entered by a doorway about twenty feet from the ground: the monks are not forbidden to furnish a ladder; but their hospitality to the weaker sex goes no further.

Passing through the wild region in which our view is taken—a tract whose only denizens are the hyena, the wolf, the jackal, and the gazelle—the route leads downwards to the plain in which so many miracles were wrought.

RAVINE OF THE KIDRON, AND CONVENT OF ST. SABA.

## XXVII.
## DESCENT TO JERICHO AND THE DEAD SEA.

Any one who would venture to travel from Jerusalem to Jericho without Bedouin protection would almost infallibly share the misadventure of the man in our Lord's parable, and fall among thieves. From time immemorial such seems to have been the custom of the locality; and in modern times the custom is recognised by the authorities, and an agreement has been concluded with the lawless denizens of the district, whereby the sum which each traveller must pay for safe conduct has been definitively settled. The black mail once paid, one or more wild Bedouins are sent with each party as evidence of the payment, and to take care that in their case the time-honoured institution of robbery is not carried out. The robbers who protect are intensely picturesque, and lend an additional wildness to the stern scenery through which they are the escort. After going round the back of the convent of St. Saba, the ride for some distance is along the edge of the precipice until the crags gradually subside into steep slopes on each side of the ravine, and it can be crossed. We traverse a succession of smooth hills, scantily clothed with grass and small shrubs, among which partridges, and groups of gazelles may be seen. Now and then a glimpse is caught of the plain to which we are descending, over a sloping table-land, bordered on each side by the rugged mountains of the wilderness, which stretches out below into spurs and ridges and peaks of strange fantastic shapes. Beyond these ridges, beyond the plain upon which they encroach, beyond and above the more distant mountain-chain, rises as it seems a fair white cloud, softened by the intervening atmosphere to pearly hue. For a mere impalpable vapour, however, it is strangely stationary: its definite outline does not change, nor do those shadows modelled in tender grey alter. Can it be snow on which we look? What alp shuts in the seething plain of Jericho? What mountain in this arid region ever bore that cool, stainless robe? It can hardly be believed, but it really is eternal snow seen through the clear air very far away; for that white cloud which refuses to move or change is the king of the Anti-Lebanon, the landmark of northern Syria, the glorious, the sacred Hermon.

Scrambling along the sides of steep defiles, always descending, until at last we get clear of the mountains, and emerging on the plain, the shore of the most mysterious sheet of water in the world is soon reached. It has been designated by many names at different epochs. In holy writ it is called "the Sea of the Plain," "the Salt Sea," "the East Sea;" by the ancients, "the Lake Asphaltites;" by the pilgrims, "the Sea of Death," "the River of Devils," and "the River that ever stinketh." By moderns it is called "the Dead Sea;" and by the Arabs, "the Sea of Lot." The whole aspect of the sea and of the surrounding objects is calculated to strike the beholder's mind with awe. The sullen waters lying heavy and motionless have a dull leaden hue, and all around is still and silent, and blasted and dead. The burning rocks of Moab's mountains and Judah's wilderness on either side, scarred and cleft by some pre-historic convulsion, are naked and barren, and do not afford a pathway even for a goat between their precipices and the sea. The blighted plain does not refresh the eye with verdure, but glares white and unfruitful, with deposits of salt. The white glistening shore is thickly strewed with drift-wood, trees, and boughs that have been torn by Jordan's floods from the thickets on its banks, swept down into the lifeless sea and cast upon its shore, where the salt-encrusted branches look like the blanched skeletons of some great herd of unknown beasts that in pre-Adamite times had perished here.

How changed is the scene from when Lot lifted up his eyes and looked down on the great plain, and saw that it was well watered everywhere, even as the garden of the Lord, and chose the fruitful land for his place of sojourn! He looked to the productiveness of the land, and to that alone, and cared not that the people among whom he meant to dwell were sinners before the Lord exceedingly. But though Lot thought too much about worldly wealth, though he was thus careless about the creed and the morals of his neighbours, and though he suffered his children to form alliances with the wicked, his heart was right towards God; and God, who saw the heart, protected him. God's mercy warned him, God's angels hurried him away from his relatives and his property; and then upon the unrighteous cities and their wicked indwellers, upon the rich and fertile vale, fell floods of fire from heaven. Four thousand years have passed since the foul smoke of that destruction, going up like the smoke of a furnace, darkened the blue sky; and for all that time the land, once so fertile and well watered, has remained blasted and parched and lifeless, the ever-enduring monument of the righteous judgment of the Almighty.

Our sketch is taken from the northern shore of the Dead Sea, looking to the south-east, along the mountains of Moab; and the contrast between the white beach covered with bleached wood and the dull purple water is very striking.

THE DEAD SEA.

## XXVIII.

## THE ACCURSED SEA AND THE SACRED RIVER.

Among the many wonders of the Sea of Lot, the greatest marvel is its extraordinary depression. Few spots, whether of land or water, are more than a few feet below the level of the earth-embracing ocean; and in one of the most remarkable instances, that of the Caspian Sea, the depression amounts only to seventy-six Paris feet. Lieut. Symonds, of the English military survey, and the United States expedition under Lieut. Lynch, have satisfactorily proved that the depression of the Dead Sea is more than thirteen hundred English feet below the surface of the Mediterranean. It is four thousand feet below Jerusalem; and its climate, and that of the great northern valley ("The Ghor") of which its basin is the termination, are totally different in character. The temperature is always high, the air sultry, stagnant, and oppressive, and the sun strikes down fierce and relentless, so that the lake wants no outlet to carry off the great body of water daily poured into it by the Jordan. For a brief space during winter floods it may overflow the flats at its southern extremity, but strong evaporation ever at work soon brings it back within its usual boundary. More or less haze always hovers over its surface, for it is an ever-seething cauldron; and sometimes the steam of rapid evaporation has been seen to rise " in broad transparent columns of vapour, not unlike waterspouts in appearance, but very much larger."

The properties of the water, its strange density and buoyancy, and its horribly nauseous taste, are among the other marked peculiarities of this monumental sea. Experience as to the first point in the unctuous fluid fully confirms the relations of travellers. It seems almost impossible to sink, and persons unable to swim in fresh or salt water elsewhere have found that here they " could sit, stand, lie, or swim in the water without difficulty." Swimmers find that they cannot make much progress, for they float absurdly high, and cannot keep their legs under water, for their limbs obstinately persist in protruding themselves above the surface. A traveller once managed to get one of his horses into the water, and says that the spectacle was extremely ludicrous. " As soon as his body touched the water he was afloat, and turned over on his side; he struggled with all his force to preserve his equilibrium; but the moment he stopped moving, he turned over on his side again, and almost on his back, kicking his feet out of water and snorting with terror." Many travellers have found unpleasant effects from the action of the water on the skin—such as redness, accompanied by smarting as if from a burn; others have only felt a slight pricking, especially in any place where the skin had been chafed. Its curious and disagreeable feel upon the skin is greasy and clammy, as if one had been bathed in oil mixed with some glutinous fluid. It is almost impossible to give in words a good idea of the nauseous taste of this slimy liquid. It is intensely salt, acrid, and pungent, and stings the tongue; and this first sensation on taking a sip is followed by an abominably bitter taste and a burning upon the lips and palate.

All that was mysterious in these strange properties of the Dead Sea water has been made clear by the researches of science. Its specific gravity has been found to be a fourth greater than that of fresh water; and it holds in solution more than a quarter of its weight of mineral salts—rather more than two hundred and sixty-four thousandths. So charged with saline ingredients is it, that it is said to be unable to dissolve common salt thrown into it. No wonder that everything its waves have moistened—sticks, stones, clay, rock, or mud—should, when dry, become snowy white and sparkling, from the crystallization of all these superabundant salts. The Arabs obtain their chief supply of salt from hence; and Irby and Mangles found them in one place peeling off a solid surface of salt several inches in thickness, and loading it on asses.

The cliffs on both sides of the sea are of limestone, but there are many indications of volcanic action in the valley, and at its southern end is Gebel Usdum, a ridge of fossil salt. Pure sulphur is found in small pieces along the shore, and is used by the Arabs to make their gunpowder. Nitre is also found, as is volcanic slag and pumice stone, so light that it floats in water. No bitumen is seen on the strand, but pieces of black bituminous stone, which partially ignites in the fire and emits a strong smell. It is said that bitumen appears in the sea only after earthquakes, and this seems the true solution. After the earthquake of 1834 a great quantity of asphalt was thrown on the south-western shore; and in 1837, after an earthquake, a huge mass of bitumen was seen floating in the sea, and at last it grounded on a shoal on the western side.

The first person, as far as we know, who launched a boat upon this sea, met with a miserable end. It was in the summer of 1835 that an Irishman, named Costigan, having determined to explore the unknown shores of the mysterious sea, had a small open boat carried by camels from the Mediterranean to the Sea of Galilee, and thence to the Dead Sea. In his tiny vessel, accompanied by one Maltese servant, he coasted the sea till he reached its southern extremity. The

THE JORDAN, SKETCHED FROM A POINT ABOVE THE BATHING-PLACE.

preparations for the rash undertaking had been mismanaged; and while they were far to the southward, water failed them. The heat was intense, and they had to row hard in the burning sunshine for two or three days to reach the northern end of the sea; but ere they touched the shore, Costigan had got his death-stroke. Years afterwards the sea was again traversed, and soundings were taken of its depths. These disclosed a remarkable feature in the bottom of the sea. Far away to the southward, a singular promontory juts out from the coast of Moab, and extends two-thirds of the way to the opposite shore, a long point running northwards for some miles in the very middle of the channel. From this peninsula, which is called by the Arabs, "The Tongue" (El Lisân), the whole sea northwards is of great depth; but from the northern part of the peninsula southward it is quite shallow—so shallow, indeed, that in seasons when the water is low, the channel between the promontory and the western coast can be forded even by donkeys. For several years, however, the water has been too deep to allow of this passage. The greatest depth of the northern portion was found to be thirteen hundred feet, and within a few yards of the eastern precipices it is more than seven hundred feet deep. The greater part of the southern portion is only two or three feet deep, and consequently the stretch of the sea to the southward varies by two or three miles, according to the season; for when the water is high, the flats are covered; and when it is low, they are beds of mud and slime encrusted with salt. The length of the sea is from thirty-eight to forty miles, and its greatest breadth is about nine miles, which diminishes to five miles at its northern extremity.

Turning northwards, and riding over the dreary plain towards the woods, which mark the Jordan's course, the river is soon reached. The change from the sweltering heat and blinding glare of the white naked plain, to the pleasant green and dark shades of the groves and thickets which fringe the shores of the sacred stream, is as delightful as it is sudden. The gloomy sea has lain as silent and motionless as death; Jordan sweeps by full of exuberant life, swift and joyous. Now with rush and ripple, freshening the sultry air by its motion, and filling it with the pleasant sound of its hurrying career; now whirling in eddies, until in some quiet nook beneath overhanging boughs, a dark pool reflects on its glassy surface the trunks of the tall trees that bend over it, and the feathery reeds whose stems it bathes.

Here, at Easter, a singular ceremony takes place, for on the Monday in Passion Week the pilgrims come down in thousands and encamp at Jericho. The Turkish governor of Jerusalem, at the head of an armed escort, marches with them to protect the unarmed multitude from the Arabs. In the dead of the night, two or three hours before dawn, the sleepers are roused by the sound of kettledrums, and then a man on horseback raises a burning torch and gives the signal for departure. Hundreds of torches are lit in a moment, watch-fires blaze up along the track, and silently the pilgrim host moves off towards the river. Their bourne is a point where there is an opening through the dense thickets, and where the shore, sloping down gradually to the water's edge, affords easy access to the stream, which during most of its course flows between steep banks. Now, in the early morning, the whole throng plunge into the river. Some go in naked, but most of them have brought from their distant homes white dresses, which, worn on this occasion, and soaked in Jordan's holy water, are carefully laid by to serve for the wearer's shroud. A single mule, horse, or camel carries nearly a whole family; and father, mother, and children all bathe together. Infants are dipped in the stream, and by their involuntary immersion derive the same benefits as those adults who have made the pilgrimage of their own free-will, and they are thus saved the expense and risk of a journey to the Holy Land in after life. Most of the throng keep near the bank, where the water is shallow and the bottom very muddy: but some, especially the Copts from the banks of the Nile, swim and sport in the strong mid-current. But while the pilgrims wash both "soul and body," and cleanse them from all impurities, material and spiritual, they not unfrequently fall victims to their zeal; for incautiously venturing too far out, they lose their footing on the slippery mud, and are carried off by the stream and drowned. When the pilgrims have finished their new baptism, they cut boughs or walking sticks as remembrances of their visit to these sacred scenes; and then, before the heat of the day sets in, they return to their encampment at Jericho. Those who visit the Dead Sea will not bathe there for fear its accursed flood should wash away all the sanctifying effect of the holy stream, and send them away from Palestine as sinful as they came.

Our sketch is taken from a point rather above the bathing place, looking up a reach of the river, which after flowing along the base of a bold bare cliff, on the shore that once belonged to Reuben's descendants, turns suddenly towards us and takes its course between two beautiful masses of rich woodland, where tall trees tower above the dense underwood that fringe the banks, which were almost concealed by the reeds that border the stream below. Then almost at our feet it turns again with a broad sweep to resume its former direction. The birds sing around in the thick covert, and the whole scene is lovely, and fresh, and pure, and charms all the more from its violent contrast to the desolate and blighted region around.

## XXIX.
## JERICHO AND THE CITIES OF THE PLAIN.

Tin bottles are made at Jerusalem for the reception of Jordan water. The pilgrims bring them down to the river, fill them, and seal them up with the intention of using the water for baptismal purposes in distant lands. For a small fee, the seal of the patriarch, or some other church dignitary, is impressed upon the corks of the metal bottles, and a regular certificate given which guarantees the genuineness of the water inside.

Returning to Jericho, from the Jordan and its sweet banks, on the way are passed the ruins called Kasr Hajla, near which is a copious spring, and these have been identified as marking the sight of Beth-Hogla (the "house of partridge"), which was one of the landmarks of the boundary between Judah and Benjamin, and belonged to the latter tribe. The ruined building was one of the convents of St. John; another, also in ruins, stands nearer the Jordan to the north. This latter was an important foundation, and very ancient, for it was built before the time of Justinian. In the twelfth century it was destroyed by an earthquake, and rebuilt; but late in the fifteenth century it was ruinous, and has so continued ever since.

The plain crossed on the way is thinly sprinkled with shrubs, and much perforated in some places by holes made by the jerboa. The village of Riha, or Eria, is the degenerate representative of ancient Jericho. It is a wretched place. The houses are mere hovels built up of loose stones taken from neighbouring ruins, and roofed with reeds, stalks of Indian corn, and brushwood, covered with stones and gravel. This roof is commonly continued over a platform in front of the dwelling, and is supported by rough poles. The whole edifice is very inartificial, and usually has a small yard attached to it, inclosed by a fence of dry thorns, in which the inmates keep their cattle at night. Heat, dirt, dust, and fever are the most salient characteristics of the place. The people are enervated by the sultry and sickly atmosphere in which they live, and are a feeble race, who do but little work. Their gardens contain only a few fig and other fruit trees, cucumbers, and a little tobacco. Most of the rich land around lies waste, but some extent of corn is cultivated by the Arabs from the high lands, who sow the seed, and in harvest time again come down to reap the corn, giving the villagers a proportion of the crop they raise, perhaps by way of rent. An old massive square tower is the only substantial building in the village. It dates probably from the time of the Crusades, and is usually garrisoned by a few Turkish soldiers. This tower is the traditional house of Zaccheus, and the view from the top of it is extensive and interesting. The inhabitants of Riha are filthy, lazy, and notoriously immoral. In or about the miserable modern village, there are no palm-trees living to remind us that here stood the strong and splendid "city of palm-trees." One solitary trunk, dead and soon to fall, with a few ragged and withered leaf-stems only remaining of its leafy crown, is the sole relic of the date groves for which Jericho was so famous.

The great vale, which includes both the plain of Jericho and the valley of Salt, is crowded with recollections of scriptural incidents, extending from the cradle of organized social life down to the close of our Saviour's earthly career; for the cities of the plain must have been among the earliest settled communities in the world.

Our first biblical glimpse of the plain is with Abraham and Lot, from the mountains above Bethel; and then we are taken to the vale of Siddim, in which stood the five cities whose kings, being defeated by the four more eastern chiefs, and Lot being carried away captive, gave rise to the only recorded deed of arms in which Abraham took part. Then finally comes the dire catastrophe, God's tremendous judgment.

"The Lord rained upon Sodom and upon Gomorrah brimstone and fire from the Lord out of heaven; and he overthrew those cities, and all the plain." No more definite information is given us by Scripture of the manner in which this judgment was carried out, and there are many hypotheses respecting it. When this extraordinary region has been more thoroughly explored, some further discoveries may perhaps be made, which may either throw light upon this obscure subject, or may furnish material for new speculations and theories. Scripture tells us all that it is important we should know. We know how steeped in iniquity were Sodom and her sisters; we know that they disregarded God's merciful warning to repent; we know that they perished by his just judgment; we know that the warning given by their fate echoes through the teaching of holy writ from the book of Genesis to that of Revelation; and finally, in entire corroboration of God's holy word, we ourselves can see the lifeless barren land, and the briny bitter flood, in the place where, before it was blasted by sin, sweet waters fertilized the delicious plain that bloomed like the garden of the Lord.

VILLAGE ON THE SITE OF ANCIENT JERICHO.

## XXX.
## PISGAH AND GILGAL.

When Israel was encamped on the plains of Moab, it was on the crest of Pisgah that Balaam stood with the king, the nobles, and the false priests of Moab around him, with the vain purpose, according to ancient custom among eastern nations, at the commencement of war, of devoting their foes, the people of Israel, to destruction by solemn rites and incantations.

But Pisgah's summit soon after saw a scene totally dissimilar. Balaam tried to evade God's command, and wished to make his spiritual gifts the stepping stones by which to reach the ends of his avarice and ambition. Moses at once bowed humbly to the will of God. Once he prayed earnestly, "O Lord God, thou hast begun to show thy servant thy greatness and thy mighty hand; for what God is there in heaven or in earth that can do according to thy works, and according to thy might? I pray thee, let me go over and see the good land that is beyond Jordan, that goodly mountain and Lebanon." God refused his petition, and from that moment Moses shows himself entirely absorbed by anxiety for the well-being, both temporal and spiritual, of the congregation he had so long governed. His next prayer to God is not for himself, but for them. "Let the Lord, the God of the spirits of all flesh, set a man over the congregation, that the congregation of the Lord be not as sheep which have no shepherd." Joshua was appointed his successor, and upon him Moses put some of his honour, that the congregation might be obedient to him.

This complete resignation of Moses to God's will is extremely touching. He had been the Hebrews' leader and guide for more than forty years of trouble and hardship. It was by his instrumentality that they were saved from Egyptian bondage. Through him was the law delivered to them. He quelled their rebellions, and interceded with God for the rebels. To him they looked in all emergencies; and now, when their toilsome pilgrimage was over, and they were on the threshold of the fertile land which was the bourne of all their wayfarings, he who had borne all the responsibility and anxiety necessarily attending such a position as his, was to have no share in the reward. Without one word of repining, the mighty prophet and leader reverently bends to the Divine decree, and passes his remaining time on earth in teaching, in warning, in encouraging, and in blessing the people he was just about to leave, and in praising the God who would still be their guide. "Ascribe ye greatness unto our God. He is the rock; his work is perfect; for all his ways are judgment. A God of truth, and without iniquity, just and right is he."

No tale in history is more affecting than that of his death at the very moment when the great object he had kept in view, and for which all his long life he had striven, was on the eve of attainment. His qualities were of the noblest kind, but not one of them was grander or more prominent than his utter forgetfulness, or rather abnegation, of self. Through all his career, his whole soul was filled with zeal for God and devotion to the people whom God had given him in charge; and to his last hour, though his own hopes were quenched in disappointment and humiliation, that zeal never cooled, that devotion never wavered. Miriam was dead, Aaron was dead, and he had no relation and fellow-worker left to climb the mountain's brow with him, and bid him farewell, as had been Aaron's lot. On Pisgah's summit, alone with his God, he saw the land beyond Jordan's stream, and there he died. The Almighty buried the corpse of his servant in a ravine of the mountain, and for thirty days Israel's children wept and mourned for their lost chief.

As we scan the undulating outline of the great eastern wall of mountains, we can see no peak that so overtops its fellows as to force us to invest it with Pisgah's name and Pisgah's associations; nor does tradition give us any assistance. As yet the position of Pisgah is undetermined; and as regards the grave of Moses, it was probably made secret by the Almighty in order that the Hebrews, so prone to idolatry, should not in after ages be tempted to adore the stern foe of all false worship, and pay divine honours at the tomb of the great teacher who so zealously inculcated the doctrine that there was but one true God. The Moslems venerate a traditional tomb of Moses, but it is placed on one of the western mountains on this side of Jordan. So sacred is the spot, that no unbeliever is allowed to enter the rude mosque which covers it.

The mourning for Moses was ended, and the ark of the covenant is borne to the brink of Jordan, while the host of Israel stands nearly a mile away from the stream, ready to follow when it moves onwards. Jordan was in flood, full to overflowing; but when the feet of the priests who bore the ark dipped in the water's brim, the Almighty, to inaugurate Joshua's mission, magnified him in the sight of all Israel, and cut off the strong stream for many a mile above where the ark stood, and from thence to the sea of the plain below left dry ground. The ark was stationed in the midst of the dry channel till all the people had passed

THE MOUNTAIN OF THE TEMPTATION.

over. On the spot where the priests stood in the middle of the river's bed, Joshua set up twelve great stones, which long remained in memorial of the miracle; and from that spot in the bed of Jordan, also as a testimony to posterity, twelve stones were taken and set up on the dry land in the place where Israel lodged that night after the passage.

The positions of the stones set up in the midst of Jordan, and those placed upon dry land, are alike undetermined; but though we cannot fix upon the exact spots where the feet of the priests stood in the mid channel, or where the twelve stones marked the central point of Israel's first resting place in Canaan, yet we may feel convinced that we have before us the scene of the miracle. The mighty host "hasted and passed over;" many miles of the river were left dry to afford them a passage, and with a broad front, in many different divisions, and at many different points along the river's course to the eastward of Jericho, they crossed the Jordan; and the plain between Eria and the stream was "the place of their encampment." At every point where we see Jordan's stream sweeping swiftly and heavily past the miracle had been enacted; the headlong career of the swollen river had obeyed its Creator's word, and in a moment checked its flow; and detachments of the multitude had passed across dry-shod from the further bank and climbed that on which we stand. The men of war of Reuben, Gad, and Manasseh led the van of Israel's host, for this was the condition upon which they had received the heritage they coveted in the land of promise.

God's law and ordinances had been delivered to Israel and fully explained, and the great lawgiver had been taken from them. Now they were to win the homes God had given them; and their leader was a man of the sword, who at the same time was filled with God's Spirit. Joshua was essentially a soldier, but a pious one; and in his character this peculiarity has been remarked, "that he is one of the few saints of Scripture, perhaps the only one, of whom no fault is recorded." This freedom from fault makes him appear less great than he really was; for "his character is overshadowed by the very greatness of the events and circumstances in which he is placed. The events are greater than the man. Hence, individually, he attracts less attention than an inferior man among events of less importance. This is not a dishonour to him, but a glory, for it shows how accurately he measured, and how truly he used his right position."

Israel's first encampment was in Gilgal, and there the Lord rolled away the reproach of Egypt off them. There the manna ceased to supply their hunger; there they got the old corn of the land; there the "Captain of the hosts of the Lord," with his sword drawn, met Joshua, who, with his strong warrior instinct, "went unto him, and said unto him, Art thou for us, or for our adversaries?"

but then, at a word, worshipped the heavenly Messenger, and loosed his shoes from off his feet, for he was told that he stood on holy ground. There Israel celebrated their first passover in Canaan. It is doubtful whether, when Israel crossed Jordan, Gilgal was a city, or merely an open place for encampment. It was about a mile from Jericho, and must have stood close to Eria, for it seems probable that Jericho itself stood rather nearer the mountain which is the subject of our illustration.

This naked and rugged peak is the traditional scene of our Lord's temptation by the devil. From the spot occupied by the small chapel which we see crowning its summit, Satan is said to have shown Jesus all the kingdoms of the world in a moment of time; and the caves and cells in its precipices were favourite abodes of hermits in the days when the anchorite life was held in esteem.

Our view is taken from the neighbourhood of the fountain whose waters Elisha healed, and which now bursts forth sweet and copious amid thickets and caves about a quarter of a mile from the mountain's base. The Jericho of the prophets stood close to this fountain. The Jericho of the New Testament is said by some writers to have been situated about a mile and a half from it. Near the spring are mounds covered with loose stones and other remains of former buildings. There are other ruins between it and Eria, and considerable remains at the mouth of the Wady Kelt, which Dr. Robinson considers to be those of the later Jericho; and some think that all these remains may have been included within the city and its suburbs. The fountain of Elisha fertilized the gardens of Jericho and Gilgal, and still waters those of Eria, and also a tract of dense thorny thicket, part of which is seen in our sketch. The ruins in the foreground are not those of Jericho, but are said to belong to sugar mills which were used here at the time of the Crusades, the sugar-cane being cultivated in the hot plain. Formerly, the ascent of the Mountain of the Temptation was a work of great merit for the pilgrim, but few attempt it now. We read that "Jesus was led *up* of the Spirit into the wilderness to be tempted of the devil." It may be that it was among the crags of the range of Marantana that he fasted forty days, and that there the tempter came to him. We have no other indications as to the locality of our Saviour's abstinence; but the "Mountain of the Temptation" may be rightly named.

## XXXI.
## JERICHO AND BETHEL.

At the time when Joshua prostrated himself before the Captain of the host of the Lord, strong Jericho was effectively beleaguered by Israel, and all external communication for its inmates was cut off. Now it was that on the threshold of their future home the Lord of hosts was about to work a strange marvel, and to help Israel with his mighty hand and stretched-out arm, almost visibly interposed in their cause, both by capturing the city they besieged, and by making the fear of his people fall on the other chiefs and armies of the land. (Joshua, chap. vi.)

Here, in after years, defiance of God's commands was severely punished, and prophecy was literally fulfilled. Jericho was cursed, Jericho was not to be rebuilt, and the penalty of disobedience was fixed.

During the lapse of ages the plain, the river, and the surrounding mountains were the scene of many important occurrences; but what more intimately concerns us as Christians claims our notice. It was to the crags of the mountain, the thickets of Jordan, the untilled places of the great plain, that multitudes from all Judæa and Jerusalem thronged to hear the voice of one who cried in the wilderness, "Prepare ye the way of the Lord, make his paths straight;" to hear the rebuke, each one of his besetting sin, and the earnest exhortation to repentance; to hear that the axe was laid at the root of the tree of works and ceremonial observances, and that a spiritual baptism, followed by a change of heart and life, was the only pathway to salvation.

In the wilds of this district, John had passed his life of privation, abstinence, reflection, and prayer, had waxed strong in the spirit, and prepared himself for his short career of important office as the herald and forerunner of Christ. Then, when the time was come in which the Holy One should enter on his mission, he came down to Jordan's bank; and John was blessed by being permitted to baptize in Jordan's stream Him whose shoe's latchet he was not worthy to unloose, to see the heaven open above his head, and the descent of the Spirit of God like a dove, to hear the Almighty Father's voice asserting the Sonship of him who had just gone up out of Jordan's stream, and to be the first to proclaim to mankind, "Behold the Lamb of God, which taketh away the sin of the world." Now,

Christ began to increase, and John to decrease. Soon John's ministry ended; and in the fortress of Machaerus, on the eastern shore of the Dead Sea, he was imprisoned for daring to rebuke a monarch's lust, and martyred to assuage a woman's revenge.

John did no miracle, but Jesus probably wrought many in this region; and two instances are on record in which his power of healing was displayed. Both were close to Jericho. On the first occasion, blind Bartimaeus sat by the wayside begging, just outside the city, when the Saviour passed. With a strong faith in the power of Jesus of Nazareth, the blind man, in spite of remonstrances, loudly cried for help; and when called, he cast away his garment, probably his only worldly possession, and went to be the subject of a healing miracle. In the other case, Christ worked by his grace upon man's soul, and by the sudden conversion of Zaccheus, and by his acceptance of the publican's hospitality, showed that his work on earth was to seek and save those that were lost.

Leaving Eria, Bethel is next to be noticed. There is no doubt that the village and ruins of Beitin mark the situation of Bethel, one of the most ancient sites in the world--the "house of God." Here Jacob, awaking out of the sleep in whose visions he had seen the ladder set upon the earth with its top reaching to heaven, the pathway of God's messengers to man, and had heard the renewal of Jehovah's promises to his fathers, exclaimed, "Surely the Lord is in this place, and I knew it not." "How dreadful is this place! This is none other but the house of God, and this is the gate of heaven."

The remains of Bethel are scattered over three or four acres, and consist chiefly of foundations and half-standing walls of houses and other buildings. In the fourth century, there was only a small village at Bethel, but afterwards it must have increased and have had a considerable Christian population, for the remains of churches still exist. One of them stands within the foundations of a much larger and more ancient edifice. In our sketch are seen the two most striking objects upon the site; the square tower, half ruined, and the vast cistern in the valley below. The latter, a true relic of ancient Bethel, is three hundred and fourteen feet long, and two hundred and seventeen feet broad. Its walls are built of massive stones, and that at the southern end is entire: the others are more or less broken down. It was partly filled by springs within its area, and these still supply the village.

From the rounded hill which forms the background of our view, Abraham and Lot looked over the plain of Jordan; and on its swelling slopes their flocks pastured when that strife arose which caused their separation.

SITE OF BETHEL.

## XXXII.
## FROM JERICHO TO SHECHEM.

The Wady Kelt is a dreary, wild ravine, which affords a passage through the mountains towards Jerusalem. The heat is stifling, and in such a climate almost any tropical plants might be cultivated successfully. There is a superabundance of heat and water; seed and skilled energy alone are wanted to make a paradise once more of this suffocating plain. It would be necessary, to be sure, to have an armed force always at hand to prevent the turbulent tribes from beyond Jordan gathering the fruits, reaping the grain, and sticking the flowers into their dirty head-gear. In the bottom of Wady Kelt is a torrent fringed with oleanders; but its precipitous sides are scorched and naked. Some think that this torrent course is "the brook Cherith that is before Jordan," where Elijah was fed by ravens. We think that it hardly fulfils the requirements of the Scripture narrative; but there seems to be no doubt that it is the valley of Achor, on the northern boundary of Judah, where the execution of Achan took place.

From hence proceeds the Ascent of Adummin, or of the red people, probably so called from some tribe of ruddy or red-haired men in the neighbourhood. Jerome says it was so called from the blood shed there by robbers who infested the pass, as they still do; and a traveller in the fifteenth century says that he saw the ruins of a castle built for the succour of travellers in that sanguinary place, and that the Germans still called the pass "the river of blood." The "going up of Adummin" is just as dangerous now as when "a certain man went down from Jerusalem to Jericho," "and fell among thieves;" and in 1820, an Englishman, Sir Frederick Henniker, was stripped, wounded, and left for dead by Arab robbers. In the precipices of Wady Kelt are many grottoes, which seem inaccessible, but which were inhabited by hermits of old. One of the ascetics who made his home here is said to have brought his body into subjection so completely that he kept himself alive upon four raisins a day. We are not told how long he lived after he restricted himself to this quantity of food.

After a succession of wild defiles and bare mountains, a fountain is reached a little below Bethany, which may be the water of En Shemesh, mentioned in Joshua. A spring near this is called the Fountain of the Apostles, and possibly it is this. At any rate it is almost certain that at this ancient source both our Saviour and his disciples often drank on their way to and from Jerusalem.

There is another road from Jericho leading directly up through a wild pass to Bethel. By this defile it was that the Israelites penetrated into the interior, taking the little city of Ai on their way. The site of Ai seems to have been recently discovered to the eastward of Bethel, the ruins consisting of heaps of large stones and some cisterns. Up this pass Elisha went on his way to Bethel when little children mocked him. Both forest and bears have disappeared.

Bireh in old times was Beeroth, a Gibeonite city, from whence the crafty inhabitants sent an embassy to Joshua. The messengers were carefully equipped in theatrical guise for the fallacious part they had to play: "They took old sacks upon their asses, and wine bottles old and rent and bound up, and old shoes and clouted upon their feet, and old garments upon them;" and their bread was stale and mouldy. They required all their shrewdness, for the Israelites had some suspicion; but the matter was settled by the appeal to their clothing and provisions. Joshua was deceived, and the people of Beeroth and the three other Gibeonite towns saved their lives and properties; for the league, enforced by oath, into which Joshua had been entrapped, was not to be broken. The Gibeonites were safe; they were reduced to serfdom, but they were to be protected from the heathen whose alliance they had deserted; and when the five kings of the south marched up here to smite the Gibeonites, Joshua fought and won in their behalf his first great battle in Canaan. Over these hills that are seen to the westward, the pagan host fled before Israel. There are many ancient remains of different dates at Bireh. The chief feature is the ruin of a fine old Gothic church, built by the knights templars, who owned the village when Jerusalem was in Christian hands.

About a mile and a half from Bireh is the Christian village of Ram Allah, whose population is about nine hundred. It is "church property"—that is to say, it belongs to the great mosque at Jerusalem, and the people pay seven hundred bushels of grain annually to the support of the Haram. Bireh is the first camping place for caravans going northward from Jerusalem; and tradition tells us that this was the place where Joseph and Mary, returning to Nazareth from the feast of the passover at Jerusalem, missed their Divine son, who was then twelve years old. It seems not unlikely that in this case monastic tradition may be right.

"A CITY OF SAMARIA WHICH IS CALLED SYCHAR."

Before reaching Bireh, some famous places are passed—Nob and Gibeon, Gibeah and Ramah of Benjamin. Among the eastern hills were Anathoth Geba of Benjamin and Michmash, and on the west were Upper and Lower Bethhoron. Over this tract the sun had stood still at Joshua's command, that Israel might make the most of their first pitched battle; and here two other great Jewish victories were won by Judas Maccabeus, and afterwards by the revolted Jews over the Romans.

Proceeding northwards, Bethel is reached. How familiar the name of Bethel is! On the hill to the east the first altar to the living God that Canaan's land saw was raised by Abraham as he passed through it for the first time; from thence he surveyed the land, and received Jehovah's promise that it should be his; and on that altar he worshipped on his return from Egypt. As Jacob slept at Bethel, under the Syrian stars, with his head upon a stone, he saw the wondrous vision, and set up that stone on the morrow as a monument to God's goodness. There he afterwards built an altar to Jehovah; and there, we are told, Deborah, the nurse of Rebecca, died, and was buried beneath an oak—the "Oak of Tears." Before all these events, there was a town called Luz in this place, so that it dates from a very early time. The stone that had served Jacob for a pillow was, according to Jewish tradition, taken to the second Temple and used as a pedestal for the ark. Hither came the people to ask counsel from the Almighty in seasons of disorganization and perplexity.

Bethel properly belonged to Benjamin, but the strong descendants of Joseph won it from the Canaanite and kept it. There is a strange mingling of true worship with idolatry in its subsequent history. When Israel separated from Judah and Benjamin, Bethel was important as a frontier fortress and sacred as a sanctuary; and here Jeroboam set up one of the golden calves to turn the heart of Israel's tribes from Jehovah's worship, and their steps from Jehovah's shrine at Jerusalem. Here took place the awful scene when the altar was rent, the ashes poured out, the king's hand withered, and the prophecy spoken, and afterwards fulfilled, of the defilement of the place dedicated to a false worship. Royal palaces and splendid shrines were also built here. Then came the Assyrian; the name of God was no longer worshipped, and lions slew the people of the land, until a priest in Bethel taught them "how they should fear the Lord." Idolatrous altar, fane, and grove were utterly destroyed by Josiah. For their desecration, the tombs were rifled of their dead, one alone being spared. In one of these rock-hewn tombs which we still see in the ravines of the eastern mountain, lay the bones of the old prophet who dwelt in Bethel side by side with those of the brother he deceived and tempted from the right path to his destruction.

Some remarkable inscription must have been placed upon it, for it caught king Josiah's eye; he was reminded of the prophecy which he was in the act of fulfilling, and he left the bones of the two prophets in peace.

Leaving Bethel and riding through winding valleys, partly cultivated, and some pretty spots luxuriant with fruit-trees and gushing with springs, the village of Ain Yebrud is reached, beautifully situated on a hill with terraced flanks, rising from wooded glens, and having a commanding view. When Stephens was in Syria, he slept here, and found a venerable old man, who had been sheikh of the village, and had resigned office in consequence of the change of affairs caused by Mehemet Ali's occupation of the country. The old man had consoled himself for his loss of dignity by taking a pretty young wife. During his previous life he had been too poor to afford more than one partner, but lately his property had increased, and he felt that he might indulge in the luxury of a second without imprudence. The helpmate of many years was consequently thrown into the background, whilst the best place in his house, and all his affections, were devoted to the juvenile bride.

"The Robber's Fountain," next following in a pretty solitary glen of evil repute. Then we look over the rich plain of El Mukhna, and then descend to its verge, and ride along the lower slopes of the western hills, till we come to the mouth of a narrow valley running down from the westward between two ranges of high hills. Turning up the glen, and in half an hour the fruit-tree groves outside the walls of Nablous are reached. The pretty spots, and all around is beautiful. There are plots of grass, and fine old trees, and rills of water, and lofty mountains furrowed by ravines and divided by a narrow strip of plain. Then, almost at the extremity of the vale, and completely embosomed in groves of fruit-trees—olive and orange, fig and vine, with many others—stands the fair city, "The Place of Sichem," "Shechem," "Sychar," "Neapolis," "Nablous," or Nabulus. Here and there a minaret, now and then a palm, rises above the flat roofs and low domes of the white town, and the orchards and gardens, supported on many a terrace, climb the mountain on whose lower slopes the city stands. It is difficult to overrate the loveliness of the situation of Nablous; and in our estimation most travellers have hardly done it justice. The range on which it is built is that of Mount Gerizim, and our view is taken from the lower declivities of Mount Ebal.

## XXXIII.

## THE MOUNTAIN OF BLESSING.

On the route from Bethel to Shechem the ancient Shiloh must have stood somewhat out of the road to the eastward. The name Seilûn is given by the Arabs as belonging to a hill covered with ruins, but they do not answer to the description of those of Shiloh, and there is no marked feature in any of the rounded hills, with their scattered rocks and stones, which often are scarcely to be distinguished from ruins, to serve as a guide from a distance to the hill on which Shiloh stood.

There is very little doubt about the authenticity of the site, for the position of Shiloh is fixed with extreme precision in Scripture, the place where the tabernacle of the Lord was first set up in Canaan. "The children of Israel assembled together at Shiloh," to receive the allotment of land for seven of their tribes on this side of Jordan. In Shiloh, Hannah made her vow, dedicating the yet unborn Samuel to God; there Hophni and Phinehas wrought evil, because "they knew not the Lord;" there Samuel ministered and communed with the Almighty; and at the gate of Shiloh, old Eli fell down and died when he heard that the ark of God was taken by the Philistines. Shiloh was destroyed at an early period, and Jeremiah says: "But go ye now unto my place, which was at Shiloh, where I set my name at the first, and see what I did to it for the wickedness of my people Israel."

Shechem, the "city of Samaria which is called Sychar," was founded long before Shiloh, and was as old as Bethel or Hebron; but, unlike them, its interest for us does not terminate with the Old Testament records, for one of the most remarkable and touching incidents related respecting our Saviour happened here.

When old Israel lay on his death-bed in Egypt, and spoke his last words of blessing to his sons and grandsons, he wittingly placed his right hand on Ephraim's head, who was Joseph's younger son, and gave him the more splendid heritage in his prophetic benediction. God made the children of Joseph a great people before they entered Canaan; and to Ephraim was given a tract of land, the very pride of Canaan, before the other tribes received their allotment on this side Jordan. Judah alone had got his territory, the wild south country; and when the general division took place in Shiloh, it was with the proviso that "Judah shall abide in their coast on the south, and the house of Joseph shall abide in their coasts on the north." To the thousands of Manasseh, and the tens of thousands of Ephraim, Moses had promised the precious things of heaven, the dew, and the precious fruits brought forth by the sun, the precious things put forth by the moon, the chief things of the ancient mountains, the precious things of the lasting hills, the precious things of the earth, and the fulness thereof; and round about Mount Ephraim now are the still-enduring evidences of how well Ephraim had fared.

The narrow valley, the place of Sichem, and the flat plain at its mouth, the plain of Moreh, where, as Abraham was on his way to his native land, he first pitched his tent for sojourning in Canaan, where the Lord appeared to him, and where he built an altar unto the Lord, was the jewel of Ephraim's inheritance. Here the fig, the vine, and the olive still thrive; of oil there is plenty, and if there is but little wine, it is because the Moslem possesses the land. The oil of Nablous is considered the best in Syria.

We read in the book of Kings that when the king of Assyria had carried the children of Israel away captive, he "brought men from Babylon, and from Cuthah, and from Ava, and from Hamath, and from Sepharvaim, and placed them in the cities of Samaria, instead of the children of Israel." The Samaritans, therefore, were strangers to the blood and religion of the Hebrews. The Assyrian monarch procured a Jewish priest who was established at Bethel to teach the heathens "the manner of the god of the land." In spite of this instruction, and though "they feared the Lord," yet they served their own gods." They adopted the Pentateuch, claimed to be co-religionists with Judah and Benjamin, and when the second temple was begun, applied for permission to assist in building it; but their request was refused and their claim disallowed, though they had intermingled with the few Ephraimites who had not been carried into captivity. Then they strove to hinder the work, and induced Artaxerxes to stop it during his reign.

Nehemiah "chased from him" a grandson of the high priest Eliashib, because he had married a strange wife, the daughter of the Persian satrap, Sanballat; and then it seems that the Samaritans got permission to build a rival temple upon Mount Gerizim, which had doubtless been one of the high places where they had worshipped their false gods. Many Jews who would not submit to the rigid interpretation of the ceremonial law, and the strict rule of Ezra and Nehemiah, threw in their lot with the Samaritans, who were regarded by the Jews with intense hatred. Shechem now became their spiritual capital;

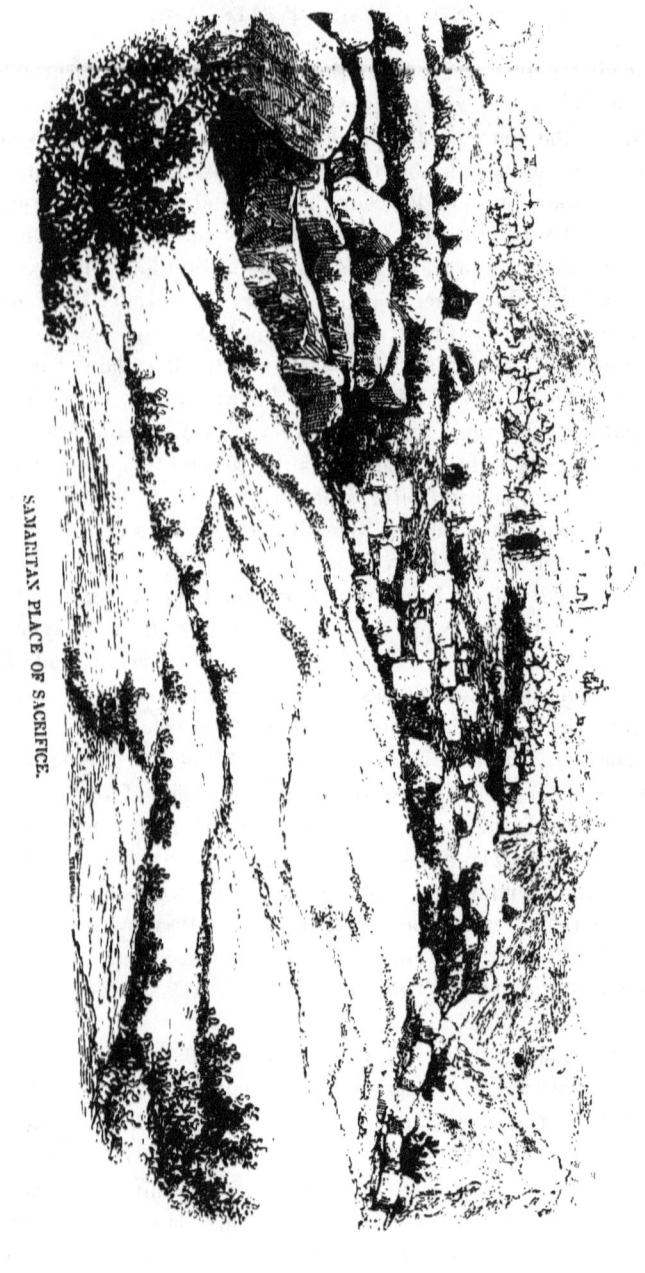

SAMARITAN PLACE OF SACRIFICE.

and when Antiochus Epiphanes threatened with death all who took part in the rites of the Jewish religion, the Samaritans repudiated their connexion with it and the Jews, and claimed to be descendants of the Sidonian worshippers of Baal. John Hyrcanus destroyed their temple on Gerizim, B.C. 129. Samaritan worship still continued to be performed there, but there is no record of the temple having ever been rebuilt.

The "Mountain of Blessing" is ascended by a steep, rough, rocky path from near the entrance of the valley. The summit of the range forms a long flattish platform, broken by some undulations, and from it the sides of the mountain fall abruptly. There are extensive remains of various kinds here, among which are what seem to be the ruins of a large ancient village; but it is on the eastern brow overhanging the plain that the most striking objects are to be seen. Here is the subject of our illustration; a smooth, bare surface of rock sloping down towards a hole leading into a natural cavern. This is the shrine of the Samaritans, profoundly venerated by them. They take off their shoes when they approach it, and turn towards it when they pray, as the Moslems do to the Kiblah. It is their holy of holies: on this rock they say that Abraham sacrificed the ram instead of his son, and that the oaks or terebinths of Moreh were in reality those of Moriah, and that this was the scene of the meeting of Abraham and Melchizedek. It seems almost certain that this was the site of the Samaritan Temple, and that the Holy of Holies stood on this smooth rock. The cave received the blood which flowed down the rock from the altar of sacrifice. Here, say the Samaritans, Jacob had his angelic vision; this is the real "house of God," Bethel; and they call the ruined village, Luz. Here the ark was placed, and the tabernacle set up. There are traces of old walls and massive stones around this rock, which probably may have belonged to the Samaritan Temple; and they most likely enclosed this peculiar rock-slope, in rivalry of the sacred rock belonging to the Temple at Jerusalem.

From the sloping rock the ground rises to a rocky knoll, on which stands a vast ruinous structure of hewn stones, which seems to have been a strong fortress. In some places the walls are nine feet thick, and the building, which consists of two adjacent parts, is about four hundred feet from north to south, and two hundred and fifty feet from east to west. At the four corners of the southern portion are square towers, and there is another in the middle of the eastern side. In the northern part is the Moslem tomb, or Wely, seen in our sketch, above the ruins of the fortress, within whose circuit it is built; and there are deep cisterns and wells among the ruins. This white tomb is seen at a great distance, and serves to mark the Mount of Blessing unmistakably from afar.

In the year 487 the Samaritans rose against the Christians, killed many of them, and maimed the bishop. As a penalty for these atrocities, they were driven from Mount Gerizim, and a church was built there in honour of the Virgin Mary. The infuriated Samaritans constantly attacked this building, and the Emperor Justinian surrounded it by a strong fortress to protect it from their assaults. There is every reason to believe that the great ruin we have just described is that of Justinian's fortress. Moses had commanded the Hebrews to set up great stones, with the law inscribed upon them, on Mount Ebal, and to build there an altar to the Lord God of Israel, and offer burnt offerings thereon. As soon as Ai was taken, Joshua did all that Moses had commanded. The Samaritans, however, will have it that it was upon Gerizim that Joshua worshipped God.

Beyond the castle is a small space of level ground, where the Samaritans encamp at the Feast of the Passover. Here, in a small area, surrounded by stones, is a trough, about four feet long, in which the bones and remains of the paschal lamb are burned, according to the command of the Jewish law, as are the handkerchiefs on which those who eat wipe their fingers when the repast is over. Near this is a circular pit, three feet in diameter, and about nine feet deep, in which the lambs are roasted, or rather baked. This pit is heated by burning wood in it, and then the lambs are suspended to a stick laid across the mouth, and so arranged that no part touches the sides or bottom. The whole Samaritan community, men, women, and children, strictly observe the ceremonial enjoined by the law, and eat the flesh "in haste with their loins girded, their shoes on their feet, and staves in their hands." Nothing will induce them to allow any stranger to their faith to taste the paschal lambs; and the Turkish governor at one time, the Arabs at another, have extorted money from the sect when assembled for the Passover, to purchase immunity from a forcible profanation of the sacred food. At length they became so rapacious that for years the sect was compelled to celebrate the feast in their own houses in Nablous.

The view from the top of the mountain is magnificent, and there is not, perhaps, to be seen in Palestine any cultivation so extensive as that of the broad plain. From the western mountains to the eastern hills which bound it, is one unbroken spread of tillage, without a fence or division. Along the spurs of the hills a wood of olives marks the site of some village; and one of the nearest of these, still called Salim, was the ancient Shalem, before which Jacob encamped when he bought "a parcel of a field" for an hundred pieces of money. On the brow of the mountain is a spot called "The Church of Adam," where Mokádá, a daughter of Adam and Eve, is reported by tradition to have been born.

## XXXIV.
## SYCHAR TO SAMARIA.

The town of Nablous is full of picturesque scenes, but the hostility of the people prevents sketching. The Moslems of this city are noted for their lawlessness and fanaticism, and have always been accustomed to abuse and maltreat all those from whose religious tenets they dissent. Christians and Jews are especially obnoxious to them: they are usually more tolerant to the Samaritans.

The small community of Samaritans which still exists in ancient Shechem at the foot of their holy mountain is the sole remnant of the sect. In the third and subsequent centuries they were scattered throughout the East in great numbers, and at the close of the fifth century they even had a synagogue at Rome, and within the last two centuries they were to be found in Egypt, in Damascus, Gaza, and elsewhere; but now they are extinct everywhere, except at Nablous, where they may number altogether about one hundred and fifty souls. They have a marked physiognomy differing much from the Jewish cast of countenance; their noses are long and straightish, complexions rather fair, lips thin, and they often have brown hair. They usually wear red turbans. They accept the Pentateuch as their sole guide in religious matters, and possess a very ancient manuscript copy, which they say was written by Abishua, the son of Phinehas, grandson of Aaron, and is consequently about three thousand three hundred years old. Some say that the real roll is never shown, except to members of the sect.

The Samaritans have tampered with the decalogue much in the same way as the Romanists have, in order to adapt God's word to meet their own views. The Romanist, to get rid of one commandment, without lessening the number of ten, splits one commandment into two; the Samaritan unites the first and second into one, and adds a tenth, which is, "Thou shalt worship the Lord thy God on Mount Gerizim."

Shechem was built in the reign of Vespasian, and then received the name of Neapolis, the "New City," and hence its present Arabic appellation, Nablous.

The only antiquities are broken columns and sarcophagi, which are used as water troughs. There is a handsome entrance to the chief mosque, which is said to have been formerly a church of the Crusaders. There are considerable soap works in the town; and, on the whole, Nablous has a thriving appearance, though there are always a number of beggars about the gates.

Riding down the valley to its entrance where a low spur of Gerizim runs out towards the great plain, we come at the point of this spur to a small mound over which some inconsiderable ruins were scattered. Great as is the interest which invests Gerizim, and famous as beauteous Shechem has been for near four thousand years, the glory of both city and mountain grows dim when viewed with the associations that dignify the sacred incidents which hallow the insignificant mound at Gerizim's roots. These shapeless ruins and a few fragments of granite columns scattered round, are all the landmarks we have, but they are undoubted, to prove that we are standing in the " parcel of a field," where Jacob had spread his tent, and which he purchased of the Shechemites. This is the parcel of ground which Jacob gave to his son Joseph, and close by the early altar called El-elohe-Israel must have been raised. In this " field," Joseph sent by Jacob to visit his brethren who were feeding their flocks in Shechem, was wandering in quest of them; here he met a man who told him where they were, and hence he went to meet the evil treatment at their hands, by which God's providence so marvellously worked out his good purposes, and which ultimately caused their preservation and advancement. Beneath these old stones is the well which Jacob dug; and on its brink sat Jesus, the way-worn, wearied, thirsting traveller, in his lowly humanity, so soon to display his Divine omniscience to convince the ignorant, unbelieving Samaritans that he was in very truth the Christ. There were souls to be saved among the despised Samaritans; and therefore Jesus, coming from Judea, " must needs go through Samaria." Hither to the Saviour came Samaria's daughter; and his words, " Give me to drink," which showed that in his breast there lurked no Jewish scorn or prejudice, disarmed hostility in hers, and won her to converse and finally to believe. Then down the valley from Shechem came the wondering disciples with the food just purchased, which the zeal to finish his Father's work prevented the Saviour from tasting; and as sitting here he then looked up that valley and saw the citizens of Shechem pouring forth to meet him, he exclaimed, " Say not ye, There are yet four months, and then cometh harvest? Behold, I say unto you, Lift up your eyes, and look on the fields; for they are white already to harvest." And now it was that the first fruits of those whom the Jews considered as strangers were gathered into the garner, soon to be followed by the great harvest

SITE OF ANCIENT SAMARIA.

of the Gentile world. Many of the Samaritans believed at once; many more when they heard him preach his gospel during his two days' stay at Sychar.

It is necessary to clamber down into a vault to look into the well. By throwing down stones it is perceived that "the well is deep," and that it is generally dry. It has been thoroughly examined; and a Hebrew Bible accidentally dropped into it by one traveller as he leaned over its margin to look down, was recovered several years after by another who lowered one of his native companions to the bottom by ropes. The well is cut in the solid rock, is nine feet in diameter and seventy-five feet deep at present, and sometimes has a few feet of water in it. Of late the vault has fallen in and stopped up the well's mouth. Christian and Moslem, Jew and Samaritan, all agree in believing that this is really "Jacob's Well;" and its position so completely harmonizes with the narratives of both the Old and New Testament that there can be no doubt on the matter. Jerome says that a church had been built over it; and the ruins round the well are those of this church, which was destroyed during the Crusades. The well is on the direct road to Sychar; and here in the sultry noontide it was natural that a tired wayfarer would rest and drink. Here our Saviour stopped after travelling up the vale where, of yore, all Israel had stood to hear the words of blessing and of cursing from the mountain ridges on either hand. The landscape has changed but little since then; and though the palaces of Sychar are gone and have left no successors, yet from a little distance, Nablous, embosomed in groves, may not differ much in general appearance from the older city.

About two hundred yards from Jacob's well, and just in the middle of the valley's entrance, we come to a small open court inclosed by a high whitewashed wall. This in an inner area, also open to the sky, contains a tomb built of masonry, with a short pillar at each end. This, according to tradition, is "Joseph's tomb," and though there is no ancient monument to mark the spot, yet it is most probable that tradition has really preserved a recollection of the true spot where the patriarch was buried. All we know for certain is, that Joseph took an oath of the children of Israel that they would carry up his bones from Egypt. "And the bones of Joseph, which the children of Israel brought up out of Egypt, buried they in Shechem, in a parcel of ground which Jacob bought of the sons of Hamor the father of Shechem," and therefore Joseph's grave must be in the immediate vicinity. The pillars at the head and foot of Joseph's tomb are reported to mark the sepulchres of his sons Ephraim and Manasseh.

In this part of the country, especially, the "coat of many colours" constantly forms a part of the native boy's dress. Men and women too, often wear it; and this gaily coloured apparel adds much to the picturesque effect of all the scenes in which figures form a prominent feature.

From Nablous the ride is along a rich valley, down which a strong stream ripples and sparkles. The fruit trees here grow to great size, and close by a fountain is a group of extraordinary fig-trees, in girth and spread of branches like forest trees. In about two hours we come in sight of the ancient capital of Israel; and in the days of its splendour, when the high and almost isolated mount it crowned was glorious with temples and palaces and vast colonnades, and girt with massive walls and lofty towers, Samaria must have seemed a grand and regal city. Its site is very commanding, but there are no imposing relics of the days of its magnificence when Herod was king. One striking ruin, beautifully placed on the brink of the boldest declivity that falls down from the platform on the hill's summit, tells of Christian rule here. This is the church of St. John, one of the most picturesque ruins in Palestine, and the one characteristic feature of Sebaste or Sebustieh, by which name the city is now called. It is the first object which catches the eye from the top of the ridge from which we first see the city; and when we descend into the valley below, it towers above on the brow of the mountain, whose base is hidden by groves of large and ancient olives. A small aqueduct crossed the road, and it is from a point just passing beneath it the view engraved in our present chapter is taken. We then climb the ascent to the wretched Arab village which desecrates Samaria's site.

The church of St. John the Baptist is said to have been erected by the Empress Helena over the grave of the martyr, but the church we see cannot have been older than the Crusades. The roof is gone, but a considerable portion of the walls remains entire, and the semicircular eastern end is almost perfect. The style of architecture is rich but rather barbarous. The interior has been partly converted into an open mosque with a tomb or wely of the " prophet John the son of Zacharias," who is greatly venerated by Mohammedans. This wely covers a chamber excavated in the rock, to which there is a descent by twenty-one steps. The tradition which places John the Baptist's tomb here is as old as Jerome, but since that epoch, the saint's place of interment and that of his imprisonment and execution have all been jumbled up together; and from about the seventh century to the present time, the imprisonment, death, and burial of the saint have all been reputed to have occurred at Sebaste, which we know is an error. Built into a modern wall inside are some marble tablets with sculptured crosses of the knights of St. John, broken and mutilated by the Arabs; and it seems likely that the church was built by that order in honour of their patron saint.

## XXXV.

## FROM SAMARIA TO EN-GANNIM.

SEBASTIYEH, the Arab name of the village which clusters round the ruined church of the Baptist, preserves the ancient appellation of the city "Sebaste," the Greek synonym given to Samaria by Herod, in honour of his patron Augustus.

There are no antique remains of importance in the village, and from the hill, which is cultivated throughout, nearly all the hewn stones and other ruins have been gradually carried off out of the husbandman's way; some piled up in the fields, and others used in making the terraces along the hill-side, or thrown into the valley below. The shafts of columns still standing in long rows are the only extant evidences of the superb structures with which Herod beautified the city he had received from Augustus as a gift. On the summit of the mount there is an open area, where stood the temple Herod raised in honour of Augustus. Here fifteen headless columns are standing, but these possibly may have formed part of a monastery and church, which are said to have once stood here.

All the columns at Sebaste are of limestone, and only one capital has been discovered after a long search by an English traveller, in the wall of a terrace. The columns sprout up out of corn-fields and gardens and amidst the vines; and in and out among them the Arab fellah drives his rude plough. There is nothing picturesque in their appearance, and they have but a monumental interest. They are the tombstones of Samaria's magnificent dead and gone. The piled-up stones among the olives in the vale below, the naked uncomely shafts upon the heights above, tell us as plainly as sculptured epitaphs could do, of Samaria and her fate. Samaria was the transgression of Jacob, and God had spoken in prophecy, "Samaria shall become desolate; for she hath rebelled against her God." "Therefore I will make Samaria as an heap of the field, and as plantings of a vineyard: and I will pour down the stones thereof into the valley, and I will discover the foundations thereof."

Samaria was not an ancient city; and though it rose to great splendour, yet in proportion to its importance its history shows us fewer features of interest than that of the other leading cities of Palestine. Its site was the private estate of an Israelite, long after the separation of the kingdoms of Judah and Israel. Then " in the thirty and first year of Asa king of Judah, began Omri to reign over Israel, twelve years; six years reigned he in Tirzah. And he bought the hill Samaria of Shemer for two talents of silver, and built on the hill, and called the name of the city which he built after the name of Shemer, owner of the hill, Samaria." His son, Ahab, built a temple to Baal here, and in his reign the city was besieged by Benhadad, the Syrian, at the head of a vast host; but whilst the Syrian leader and " the thirty and two kings that helped him " were drinking themselves drunk in their pavilions, a small band of two hundred and thirty-two young men went out of the gates of Samaria, in obedience to the word of one of God's prophets, and utterly routed the beleaguering army.

To Samaria Ahab was brought in his chariot dead; and at the pool there, in accordance with Elijah's prophecy, dogs licked up the monarch's blood. Again, Benhadad besieged the city for the long space of three years, and a fearful famine within the walls was the result; and whilst silver was valueless in comparison with even the most loathsome food capable of sustaining life, we are told of the horrible story of the two Samaritan mothers and of their compact to kill and eat their infants in turn. No wonder that in the face of such an awful visitation, and when appealed to by one mother to make the other perform her part of the frightful agreement, even the wicked Jehoram was found to have privately humbled himself before God; and when he rent his clothes in horror at what he heard, it was observed that beneath his royal robes he wore the sackcloth of humiliation upon his flesh. Then, for the third time, the Syrian host was discomfited by a direct miracle before the city, and four lepers, who were at the gate, found the besieging camp deserted, and its spoils undefended; and in Samaria's gate the lord, who scoffed at Elisha's prophecy of sudden plenty, met the fate the prophet pronounced upon his incredulity, and was trodden to death by the starving multitude as they rushed forth upon the Syrian prey. In the year B.C. 720, the Assyrians took the city and colonized it. In later times, Philip preached at Samaria with success, and wrought miracles, numbering amongst his nominal converts, Simon the sorcerer; and to Samaria Peter and John were sent to lay hands upon the newly made Christians that they might receive the Holy Ghost.

Leaving the city of Omri and of Herod, descending into the deep valley which surrounds it, and climbing a steep rocky hill, in about three quarters of an hour the prettily situated village of Burka is reached. Fine groves of old olive trees cover the hill-sides; and as we scramble up a narrow rocky path to

EN-GANNIM, THE PLAIN OF ESDRAELON, AND THE MOUNTAINS OF GILBOA.

the summit of a high ridge beyond, we have a succession of beautiful and interesting views. Passing near some picturesque villages, we descend to a fertile plain almost circular, and about three or four miles across. This is "the drowning meadow," so called because it forms a basin from which there is no outlet for the streams that fall into it in winter. Their waters consequently collect and form a shallow lake, and the moisture it retains even in summer causes the plain to yield abundant crops. The low hills which surround it rise abruptly from its level expanse. They are covered with brushwood; and on the top of the boldest of them stands the ruined fortress of Sânûr, the stronghold of a family who ruled the neighbouring country with the strong hand in spite of sultan or pacha. They were a brave, unscrupulous set, and many an unsuccessful attempt was made to subject or suppress them, but they held their hill-fort in spite of several sieges of some months' duration.

About the close of the last century, Djezzar Pacha, of Acre, a monster of wickedness and cruelty, besieged Sânûr for two months, and had he captured it would probably have massacred all its inhabitants, and appropriated their possessions; but he was repulsed. In 1830, the sheikh of Sânûr openly rebelled against Abdallah Pacha, who then governed Syria, and was besieged in consequence. The famous chief of the Lebanon, the emir Beshir, was summoned with his mountaineers to assist in the attack, and after a siege of four months the walls were breached and the castle carried by assault. Since then the dispersed members of the family and their retainers have collected among the ruins of their ancient stronghold, and gradually rebuilt its walls, in the hope that some day or other they may be able to resume their old state of predatory independence and defy the Turk and the law.

From the top of the ridge above "the drowning meadow" we look down upon another little plain, and on its southern side see a green mound, which still bears the name of Dothan. There seems to be no doubt that this is the fertile vale in which Joseph's brethren were feeding their flocks when he sought them at Shechem; and when he followed them hither and found them, it was here that they first cast him into some empty cistern, and afterwards drew him out and sold him to the Ishmaelite merchants, whose caravan of spicery, and balm, and myrrh passed by on its way from Gilead to Egypt.

In the town upon that little hill Elisha dwelt, when the Syrians were at war with Israel; and knowing beforehand by inspiration all the plans of the Syrian commander, divulged them to Israel's king, who acted upon this information, and "saved himself there not once nor twice." "The heart of the king of Syria was sore troubled for this thing," and he suspected treachery among his own people; but one of them telling him of Elisha's prophetic power, he sent spies to find out the residence of the prophet. "And it was told him, saying, Behold he is in Dothan," and he laid his plans for the prophet's capture. Then, when Elisha's servant rose early in the morning, he saw the city surrounded by a Syrian host, with horses and chariots, and cried out, "Alas, my master! how shall we do?" The answer was, "Fear not; for they that be with us are more than they that be with them." The young man's eyes were opened, and then he saw the host of the Lord, the chariots and horses of fire, circling round the Lord's chosen servant for his protection. Then another strange miracle was wrought in that green plain; for the Syrian leaders and soldiery, all struck with blindness, were led by Elisha to Samaria, and when their sight was restored to them, found themselves altogether in the power of Israel's king. "My father, shall I smite them? shall I smite them?" cried out the monarch; but Elisha's prisoners were not to be thus treated, and the prophet answered, "Wouldst thou smite those whom thou hast taken captive with thy sword and with thy bow? Set bread and water before them, that they may eat and drink, and go to their master." The king obeyed, "prepared great provision for them," and then sent them away unharmed.

From the broad shoulder of the mountain from which we look upon Dothan, we descend to the village of Kubâtiyeh, a fine prosperous village, inhabited by a set of notorious rascals, who have long been in the habit of robbing every solitary traveller they fall in with; nor are small caravans safe unless they are well armed and show a bold face.

We are now in the territory of Manasseh; and in these deep valleys leading down from the central mountain range of Ephraim to the great plain of Esdraelon, the horns of Joseph, the ten thousands of Ephraim and the thousands of Manasseh, pushed the people who came in armed array against the inheritance of him that was separated from his brethren.

Jenin represents the ancient En-gannim, "the fountain of gardens;" and to this day the name is quite appropriate. Placed on a slightly rising ground, on the very border of the great plain, and surrounded by a belt of gardens well watered, and very productive, it speaks aloud of beauty and of plenty. The houses are well built of stone, the mosque is of considerable size, and the people seem well off. A sparkling stream of clear water flows through the village, and then diffuses itself through the gardens, which are protected by strong fences of prickly fig. One graceful group of lofty palms just outside the village, and single trees here and there rising above the gardens, combine with the masses of cactus to heighten the oriental effect of the view.

In our sketch, an arm of the great plain is seen behind the town, and is bounded by the range of Gilboa's mountains.

## XXXVI.
## THE GREAT PLAIN AND JEZREEL.

The Plain of Esdraelon, whose name is merely the Greek form of the Hebrew word Jezreel, is so called from the old royal city of Jezreel, situated near its eastern extremity on a low spur running out from Mount Gilboa. This broad plain stretches its arms across the middle of Palestine, from the Mediterranean to the Jordan: its central portion is almost triangular, the southern base being about eighteen miles long, the eastern fifteen miles, and the northern about twelve. Only a small portion of its expanse is tilled, though the soil is wonderfully fertile, to which fact gigantic weeds and huge strong thistles bear testimony. Three branches run out to the eastward. The southernmost branch lies between the uplands of Manasseh behind Jenin, and the mountains of Gilboa; the northernmost runs between Mount Tabor and the Lesser Hermon; and the central branch between the latter range and that of Mount Gilboa; and this is both the richest and most famous. This is the "Valley of Jezreel," where Gideon conquered, and Saul and Jonathan met defeat and death. At each side of its western entrance stood Shunem and Jezreel; and far down it to the eastward was Bethshan, now called Beisan, which looked down into the Jordan valley, and upon whose walls, which the Hebrews had never been able to win from the Canaanite, the bodies of Saul and his sons were fastened. There they hung till the mighty men of Jabesh-Gilead, a city situated nearly opposite Bethshan on the other side of Jordan, carried them off from their ignominious position, and buried them. It was a feeling beyond mere respect for their slain king which prompted the warriors to this daring feat. They were paying a tribute of genuine disinterested gratitude for past benefits to one who never could thank or repay them.

The great plain was the inheritance of the tribe of Issachar, and En-gannim was within its boundary. Old Israel on his death-bed had prophesied: "Issachar is a strong ass, couching down between two burdens; and he saw that rest was good and the land that it was pleasant, and bowed his shoulder to bear and became a servant unto tribute;" and Moses in his farewell blessing had said, "Rejoice, O Issachar, in thy tents." The character of the tribe was modified by the character of his country. The plain was so indefensible, so open to sudden incursion from all quarters, that Issachar preferred to purchase peace from whatever power might, for the moment, be in the ascendant by the payment of black mail, to keeping himself prepared at all times to fight for his freedom and his wealth. He had few cities of any importance; consequently he led chiefly a nomad life, dwelling in tents; and the fat soil of the land that he saw was pleasant, gave him ample means of paying the exactions of his masters whoever they might chance to be, and of growing rich himself besides. Few were the occasions in which he took a definite political course; and when he did, he seems to have understood and appreciated the exigencies of the moment and acted with prudence.

From the dawn of history this plain has never been safe ground: its wealth has ever invited inroad. The Canaanite drove over it in his iron chariots at one time, and for a period from the Philistine fortress at Bethshan the marauder often went forth to the spoil; but, at intervals, for the whole of its history down to the present moment, "the children of the East," the wild tribes from beyond Jordan, have come up "with their cattle and their tents, as grasshoppers for multitude, both they and their camels without number, and have entered into the land to destroy it." They and the Midianite reaped what Israel had sown; and now year by year, to a greater or less degree, they pour over the Jordan with all their families and property, feed their flocks on the wild pasture land, and reap much of what the Arab fellah has sown. In the open plain there are no villages, but here and there we see a cluster of the black tents of the Bedouin and their herds scattered around.

This plain was the natural battle-field of Palestine, though not one which the Hebrews would have chosen, being more suited to those who trusted in chariots and in horses, which formed no part of Israel's array. Here Israel won some of his greatest victories. The battle that inspired the triumphant hymn of Deborah was fought here, and here the host of the children of the East was so miraculously discomfited by Gideon. For seven years the Midianites and their allies had ravaged the territory of Israel by God's permission. At length, "the children of Israel cried unto the Lord;" and he gave a ready answer to their prayer, and sent his angel to commune with Gideon face to face, and gave him his mission to save his country. To strengthen his faith, strange signs were vouchsafed to him; and when he had gathered together an army of thirty-two thousand men from his own tribe of Manasseh and from Asher, Zebulun, and Naphthali—Issachar, which lay in the midst of these tribes, being left out—the Lord, who could save by many or by few, saw fit to use the latter as his instrument, and the mighty deliverance from their oppressors was effected by three hundred chosen men of Israel.

THE CITY OF JEZREEL, AND THE LESSER HERMON.

The most pathetic dirges over the mighty dead which Scripture hands down to us were sung in grief for defeats which Israel suffered in Esdraelon's plain.

Almost on the same spot where Gideon triumphed over the Midianite, Saul was vanquished by the Philistines, but now it was up the bare steeps of their own familiar mountains that the defeated fled for refuge; for the Israelites were essentially mountaineers, and among precipices and defiles alone could they hope to escape the pursuit of those who were wont to drive iron chariots in the plain. On Mount Gilboa, Israel fell down slain, and Saul and Jonathan were not divided in their death.

Directing our course northwards along the border of the plain, right across the opening of the three eastern branches, our first point is Jezreel, now called Zerin; and here, though there is much to think of and recall, yet there is little to see. A great ruinous square tower, many artificial caves now used by the villagers as granaries, several sarcophagi, some of which are ornamented with sculpture, and some heaps of rubbish, are the only relics that connect Zerin with the past in which Jezreel played for a time so conspicuous a part. About twenty modern hovels are scattered over this ancient site. The tower is used as a place of entertainment, where it is said that native travellers "are treated to bare walls, fleas *ad libitum*, and a supper at the public expense." This tower cannot be the "Tower of Jezreel," commemorated in Scripture, but it may be its successor, built on the same foundations; and it is remarkable that the only prominent feature on the site should be just such a tower as that on which the watchman stood who spied the company of Jehu as he came, and said, "I see a company," and reported the subsequent occurrences until he could identify the leader by his furious driving.

Our sketch is taken from the south, and from this point of view we cannot appreciate the fine position of the ancient city, which seems, as seen from hence, to have covered a low rocky mound elevated but little above the undulating plateau by which it is approached; but on the northern side there is an abrupt descent of more than a hundred feet to that famous part of the plain which is specially called the Valley of Jezreel. The prospect from the river in Jezreel, therefore, was a wide one, and Jehu's company could be seen from afar as they hurried up this centre branch from the ford of Jordan. The naked peak and weather-worn sides of Lesser Hermon are well seen in our view; and when Israel encamped at the base of Gilboa, by the fountain of Jezreel, at the bottom of the steep descent from the city, and Philistia's forces were collected at Shunem at the foot of Little Hermon on the opposite side of the valley, Saul, troubled in mind because he felt the Lord had forsaken him, and that there was no prophet to give him encouragement and advice, went in disguise by night over the mountain's shoulder to Endor to consult the woman who had a familiar spirit.

Jezreel was an ancient city mentioned in Joshua, but for its magnificence and its historical celebrity it was indebted to Ahab, who for a time raised it to the importance of a provincial capital for Israel. The royal residence of Judah's sovereigns was always at Jerusalem, but Israel's monarchs changed their regal abodes according to individual fancy. Jeroboam first beautified Shechem and dwelt there, and afterwards seems to have built Tirzah, whose loveliness was a proverb, but whose site is unknown. Nadab probably made it his residence: Baasha reigned there twenty-four years; and his son, Elah, two years, until he was assassinated whilst he was "drinking himself drunk" in his palace there. In Tirzah, the short sovereignty of Zimri was spent, and he perished in the flames of the burning palace which he himself had set on fire. Omri, we have seen, founded Samaria, and Ahab built his ivory house at Jezreel, which was then, doubtless, surrounded with groves and gardens, among which was that small plot inherited from his ancestors by Naboth, coveted by Ahab, and won, we well recollect how, by Jezebel. This small garden, and the sad tale of the wronged citizen who owned it, have done more to fix the name of Jezreel in the popular mind than all the other events transacted there put together.

A fountain not more than a mile from Zerin, that from which the inhabitants usually draw their supply, is probably the famous "Fountain of Jezreel," where Saul and Israel encamped before the great disaster of Mount Gilboa; and is thought to be identical with the spring of Harod where Gideon rested before his attack on the Midianites. The spring bursts forth with a fine strong stream at the foot of some rocks at the bottom of the steep descent into the Valley of Jezreel.

## XXXVII.
## FROM JEZREEL TO TIBERIAS.

The first Hebrew who viewed Esdraelon's Plain must have looked on many a scene identical with that which is now spread out before our eyes. The barrenness of Little Hermon contrasted as violently then as it does now with the exuberant fruitfulness of the level ground around its base; and this fertile soil is now tilled as rudely by the Arab as it was then by the Canaanite. The wide tract, untouched by the plough, is covered with the same vigorous herbage, and throws up the same rank weeds as when it fed the flocks and herds of the "people of the East," who were attracted by its pasturage from the further side of Jordan. The dark tents of the Arab encampment we see far off have in no way changed in appearance and construction since the hoary patriarchal times, and such tents were ancient in Joshua's day. The stream that gushes with pleasant murmur from the foot of the rock that shades us, spreads out into a pool, and then ripples cheerily along as if in laughing defiance of the fierce heat and lurid sunshine. Thirsty animals—sheep, goats, horses, asses, were drinking along its course. The women, who now dwell on Jezreel's ruins, dress in much the same costume as those who dwelt there of yore, and like them, believers in a false creed, fill water jars at the spring; and girls who might have been Midianite damsels sit with their feet in the stream dabbling and splashing with the water which soon becomes tepid after it leaves its birthplace in the rock. There is a gradual slope upwards from hence to the base of Little Hermon; and the village over the swelling brow is the ancient Shunem, a town when Joshua invaded the land, and the camping place of the Philistines on that night when Saul sought the wise woman of Endor, and his army slept around; whilst the ridge just behind the village is no doubt the "Hill of Moreh," where the Midianites were posted when Gideon and the three hundred went up from this "Well of Harod," and "the sword of the Lord and of Gideon" overthrew Israel's oppressors. There is not an object that speaks of the nineteenth century in all we see around us; not even the living Arabs themselves, according to the following sketch, by a traveller, of an incident occurring at this very spot:—

"Just after we had halted here, a sheikh of one of the wild Eastern tribes, in dress and ornaments, bearing and habits, just such another as one of the 'kings' or 'princes' of Midian, rode up upon a fine mare richly caparisoned, which had a foal running at her side. He might have been Oreb, or Zeeb, 'The Raven,' or 'The Wolf,' or perhaps even as great a chief as Zebah or Zalmunna. He dismounted by the fountain, and, after a short parley with our servant Salem, came up, and courteously bade us welcome; then sitting down he partook of our 'bread and salt,' which, in this particular instance, consisted of coffee, cake, and tobacco. When we were about to continue our journey he gave us a pressing invitation to pass the night at his tents, which were pitched a little out of our road. We excused ourselves on the ground that our baggage and tents had long gone on, and could not now be recalled. He urged us then, at any rate, to dine on our way; but knowing something of Arab feasts and of the time it takes to prepare and get through them, and then sit smoking afterwards, we were obliged to decline this offer of hospitality, which would, to a certainty, have prevented our reaching our tents that night. The sheikh then insisted upon holding our stirrup as we mounted our horses, and we bade him farewell.

"When we had ridden for some distance over the plain, we saw an Arab galloping to cut us off, and soon he came up with us. Imagination could not picture a more poetic embodiment of the Arab and his attributes, in face, form, manners, sumptuous attire, and splendid steed, than the beautiful boy, who now with all the grace of a high bred Oriental, accosted us in phrases of Eastern politeness as ancient as the patriarchs. 'You are welcome; will you do us honour? will you be our ally?' This was the young sheikh, the son of our acquaintance at Jezreel's fountain, and he had been despatched after us by his father to try, by importunity, to persuade us to be his guests. His head and shoulders were covered with a flowing Mecca handkerchief of red and yellow silk and gold, with a long fringe which fell over his white robe, and his boots were scarlet. He held, and managed well, an immensely long spear, and his white mare was richly caparisoned with scarlet trappings covered with tassels and ornaments. With an earnest face and most winning smile, he begged us to turn aside with him, if it were only for an hour, to drink coffee; but we were obdurate, and at last he turned back disappointed. His whole appearance stamped him as being of high degree, the scion of some ancient warrior race of unmitigated robbers, possibly a descendant of those very 'kings,' who, as Scripture tells us, met their deaths so calmly and bravely at Gideon's own hands, as became such high-born leaders in the battle and the foray."

Leaving the fountain, we turn back to a little spring beneath the town of Jezreel. It was somewhere near this that Naboth's property lay, and in this

TOWN AND LAKE OF TIBERIAS, WITH MOUNT HERMON IN THE DISTANCE.

"portion of Naboth the Jezreelite," part of the prophecy which denounced the house of Ahab was fulfilled to the letter; and king Joram, Ahab's son, was slain by Jehu, and cast into "the plat of ground," to gain which the wickedness had been done. Then, on the ridge above, retribution fell on the chief actor in the crime, and dogs ate Jezebel in the portion of Jezreel, according to Elisha's word.

Sôlem, the ancient Shunem, is now a large village, defended, as well as its gardens of orange and lemon trees, pomegranates and olives, by dense and lofty hedges of prickly fig, an impenetrable barrier to man and beast. Here dwelt the wealthy lady who entertained Elisha as often as he passed, and, with her husband's sanction, built a little chamber on the wall of their house, opening upon the terrace roof, and placed it at the prophet's disposal. Here, as a reward, a son was given to the childless pair; and when years had passed, in the fields around the boy got his death stroke and died in his mother's arms in Shunem. The Shunemite had shown her love for God and God's servant. Now her faith was sorely tried, and found to be true and unwavering. In her hour of dire distress she sought Jehovah's servant, and the son that had been given as the reward of her love was given again to the faith that could believe even in the face of death; and in the village through which we pass, her dead son was raised by the prophet.

As we ride on, we see a little to our right a smaller, poorer village on the northern base of Little Hermon. Here, too, the dead was raised to life; but it was one who was greater than a prophet who wrought the miracle. This village is still called by the same name as when Jesus passed this way and met at its gates the bier of the dead man who was the only son of his widowed mother. This is Nain; and here He who was the resurrection and the life, in compassion for mortal sorrow, broke the bands of death and gave back the dead son to his mother. We are now crossing the entrance of the northernmost of the eastern branches of the plain; and the strange mass of Tabor, rounded and vast, rises before us, while down the eastern valley we see another poor hamlet of about twenty hovels. This is Endor. The village of Deburieh, at the foot of Mount Tabor, marks the site and preserves a recollection of the name of Daberath, a city of Issachar, on the very border of Zebulon, and allotted to the Levites, as was also En-gannim at the other extremity of the plain.

Every one of the Scriptural sites we have referred to in the plain of Esdraelon claims a high antiquity, but one alone of them is famed in the Gospel narrative. Jesus must often have crossed the plain on his way to and from Nazareth and the other Galilean cities where he passed so much of his earthly career; but at Nain alone, one of the least important of the towns of Esdraelon, is it recorded that he did any mighty work. Nain now is wretched and ruinous;

but the sweet remembrance of the touching story of the widowed mother's grief and the Saviour's tender sympathy gives a more living interest to the poor hamlet at Little Hermon's feet, and the sepulchral caves in its hill-side to which the dead man was being carried, than we can feel for lordly Jezreel, or for the old and strong fortress city of Bethshan.

Mount Tabor is climbed through oak forests and thorn thickets, among which, upon the level summit, are open grassy glades, amid whose thick flower-spangled herbage coveys of partridges nestle and gazelles browse. Around this extensive platform are the substantial remains of ancient fortifications and other ruins; and the cool shade of the trees and the invigorating breeze that sweep around the mountain's brow are doubly delightful after the heat of the plain. The views from this platform are splendid, whether from its southern margin looking over the southern country, or over Galilee of the Gentiles. Mount Tabor is the traditional scene of the transfiguration of our Lord; but various circumstances combine to show the improbability that this glorification of the Son of man could have occurred on the broad platform which crowns this grand and isolated mountain. One fact seems almost conclusive upon the point: Jesus took Peter, and James, and John, the apostles he most loved and trusted, " up into a high mountain apart;" but Tabor's top was then no place for solitude. A walled city covered the level area both before the New Testament days and long afterwards. Jerome hints a doubt on the correctness of the tradition; but long after his day convents and churches were built, and pilgrimages made to this holy mountain, and no one doubted that it was the real scene of the glorious event. Mount Tabor is famous in history, and has seen many a battle, from the great victory of Barak to that of Napoleon.

Looking down from the lofty ridge, the Lake of Tiberias is seen in its whole expanse outspread far beneath. From the sketch engraved in our present chapter an idea may be formed of the dilapidated aspect of the town and its defences—fallen walls, breached towers, a ruinous castle, and a mosque with its cupola shattered and gone. It was not man who worked all this destruction, though the fortifications of Tiberias look as if they had just been stormed and dismantled by some conqueror. The earthquake of the 1st of January, 1837, was the irresistible foe which prostrated wall and tower, and there the ruins remain as nature's convulsion left them.

On the flat roofs of most of the houses there are arbours or tents made, some of straw, others of boughs of trees, or of branches of oleander, as summer bed-rooms for the inhabitants. Beyond the town the lake is seen bounded by the inhabitants of Bashan, high above which snowy Hermon, still far distant, towers aloft.

## XXXVIII.
## GALILEE OF THE GENTILES.

Tiberias is esteemed a holy city by Israel's children, and has been so dignified ever since the middle of the second century. For five or six hundred years it was the metropolis of the Jewish race, and on the slopes outside the town many of their most revered rabbis were interred. Next to the Valley of Jehoshaphat, the dying son of Abraham would wish to rest on this bleak upland. The old castle of Safed crowns an isolated peak to the north-west of Tiberias, and rises more than three thousand feet above the lake. Around it the town hangs on the precipitous mountain side, and is counted as one of the four sacred cities of the Hebrews.

In 1837, a horrible catastrophe befel Safed. The whole town and castle were destroyed by an earthquake, but the Jewish quarter, built as we described, met with an awful fate. The topmost row of houses fell down on the next, and their combined ruin again on the third rank, and so on, till the whole quarter had crashed down and was heaped upon the inhabitants and their property. Five thousand persons were supposed to have perished at Safed, and four thousand of these were Jews.

The "sermon on the mount," the first teaching given by our Lord to his apostles after their appointment, and meant more specially for their instruction than for that of the multitude, who also heard and were astonished at the new and wonderful doctrine, was delivered from one of the hills in this neighbourhood; and if the traditional site, "The Horns of Hattin," called by pilgrims "The Mount of Beatitudes," be the true one, Safed was full in view; and it may be that our blessed Saviour made use of this city enthroned on its towering peak as an emphatic illustration of his meaning when he said, "A city that is set on a hill cannot be hid."

What the city then in existence was we do not know. There are old foundations on the peak; and it is most probable that such a splendid site was occupied in our Lord's day as it was afterwards. The castle most likely was built by the Crusaders: at any rate it was held by the Knights Templars, and was so strong that Saladin besieged it for five weeks before he could take it. It is a striking object from all the country round. It looks over the whole of the

Lake of Tiberias, over all the ancient kingdom of Bashan east of the Jordan valley, and over the greater part of Galilee, and seems to be about on a level with Mount Tabor.

A few miles north-west of Safed is the village of Meiron. Here, among other sacred tombs, is that of Hillel, said to have been the grandfather of Gamaliel. To these shrines, some time in the month of May, Jewish pilgrims flock in thousands and celebrate strange heathen rites in honour of the great saints buried here. This festival, which is called "The Feast of the Burning," and appears to be some modification of the worship of Moloch, is carried on amid singing, dancing, feasting, drunkenness, and immorality. Then, when the revel is at its height, pilgrims burn all kinds of valuables. Costly shawls, silk robes, rich embroidery, books, scarfs, handkerchiefs, are dipped in oil and set on fire amid screaming trills from the women, with shouts and clapping of hands which grow more uproarious whenever any particularly costly article is consumed, or when something makes a greater blaze than is usual! The object of these pagan orgies is probably to win the intercession and buy the protection of the holy men around whose graves they are perpetrated; and we may infer that it was the vicinity of these tombs which drew the Jews to Safed, and caused that modern town to be ranked with the ancient cities of Tiberias, Hebron, and Jerusalem, though we have no positive evidence on the subject.

At Tiberias about six hundred persons were killed during the earthquake; and now the population has dwindled down to about two thousand, half of whom are Jews.

We are now in Galilee; and to the Galilean ministry of the Saviour the records of the first three evangelists are in a great measure devoted. It was natural that this should be so, for it was in the country and cities of Galilee that Christ preached his own gospel during the greater part of his ministerial career; and the district of Galilee which was most favoured by his frequent presence and miracles was unquestionably this "Sea of Galilee which is the Sea of Tiberias," on whose shores we now are, and the land bordering upon it to the northward. The Hebrews of his own race, the royal tribe of Judah, would none of him; Benjamin, Ephraim, and Manasseh, who were less of kin to him than the other tribes, being sprung from lonely Rachel, were as stiff-necked as Judah; and the sure word of prophecy had spoken: "The land of Zabulon, and the land of Nephthalim. . . . . Galilee of the Gentiles; the people which sat in darkness saw great light." Not a tittle of God's word could fail; and therefore in Galilee, to the multitudes of Zabulon and Naphthali, Christ himself preached salvation and healed their sick in crowds.

THE FOUNTAIN OF THE VIRGIN AT NAZARETH.

The northern part of the lake is specially connected with his ministry. The level strand between the mountains of Naphthali and the lake lead to the "Land of Gennesareth." Mejdel still preserves in Arabic garb its old name Magdala. Here was born Mary the afflicted sinner, Mary the healed and loving convert, who stood by the cross of the dying Saviour who had taken her from Satan's thrall, Mary who was the first of all his followers to find that her dead Lord was risen, and the first to whom that risen Lord appeared triumphant over death.

Few and wretched are the huts of Magdala at the southern extremity of the fertile plain of Gennesareth, but they are the only fixed dwellings of men throughout its whole extent, which Josephus described as being in his day an earthly paradise, exulting in eternal spring. Even now, in its desolate state, it repays by a lavish yield the slight and careless toil which the rude Arab peasant expends upon it here and there in patches; and still does a broad fringe of graceful oleanders border the strand; but more prominent are the tangled thickets of lote tree, the mighty thistles, the coarse grass, and rank weeds, wide spread over the plain, which, when Christ dwelt here, was one prolific garden.

There is almost nothing to see at the ruins of what weighty authorities believe to have been Capernaum, for thorns and thistles almost choke and hide the fallen stones and indistinct foundations of the city whose buildings were anciently grouped about the modern Khan Minyeh and the fig-tree fountains. Are these the remains of Capernaum? Who can tell? About the "Land of Gennesareth," about Magdala the birthplace of Mary the Penitent, and about Roman Tiberias, there is no doubt; but all local recollections, all reliable tradition respecting Capernaum, Bethsaida, and Chorazin, have passed away. One of the three cities must have occupied this site, and it may probably have been Capernaum; but we have no certain evidence that the home of Christ during his ministry, "his own city," stood here. We know that we tread on the ground where the Redeemer walked and taught and meditated, and wrought miracles. About us are "the cities wherein most of his mighty works were done," but who for all that "repented not." On that smooth beach which stretches for three or four miles on each side of us, Peter and Andrew, James and John, heard the gracious call of Him whom the winds and the storm obeyed, and abandoned on that strand their boats and nets and livelihood.

There again and again Jesus landed and embarked; there the multitude was gathered while he taught them out of a ship; and there the crowd was reproved who followed him for the sake of the perishable food, and not for the meat which endureth unto everlasting life. In Galilee, not far from hence, Christ wrought his first recorded miracle, and this shore of Galilee's sea saw the last. On this smooth beach, where first he called them, the glorified Son of man, after having perfected our salvation, again appeared to his apostles, busied with their work as of yore; and ere they knew him he did one more miracle akin to his mighty works of old. John was the first who recognised his risen Lord, but zealous Peter dashed through the water first to meet him. The unbroken net "full of great fishes an hundred and fifty and three," was drawn to land, and from their Lord's hands the hungry fishermen received the food miraculously supplied.

As we look around us on this spot, we seem to hear the prophetic doom echoing through eighteen centuries. "Woe unto thee, Chorazin! woe unto thee, Bethsaida!—And thou, Capernaum, which art exalted unto heaven, shall be brought down to hell." And must we not believe that the blotting out of their place and name so utterly from human recollection formed part of the fulfilment of the Saviour's words of sorrowful denunciation?

Our northward course ends here. A village named Keffr Kenna is thought by some to be Cana of Galilee, and ancient tradition favours the idea. Modern research, however, has discovered another village a few miles further north which equally answers the Scriptural requirements, and corresponds more exactly in name with the scene of the miracle. It is called "Kana-el-jelil." We cannot decide to which village the honour belongs, for their claims seem equally balanced.

Belonging to Nazareth there are two genuine antiquities, a fountain and a tradition. In our engraving we have portrayed the one, and represented in the background a building raised to commemorate the other.

The low plain edifice beyond the fountain is the Greek church of the Annunciation, erected here because, according to tradition promulgated in the spurious gospel of the Redeemer's youth, Mary the Virgin was drawing water at this fountain when, from the mouth of the angel Gabriel, she heard the first words of prophetic salutation, "Hail! thou that art highly favoured!"

Thither the women and girls of Nazareth, with long white veils and bands of coins over their heads, throng to fill their graceful water-jars. Their veils do not cover their faces, many of which are beautiful. To this very fountain, in olden time, may have come Mary, the mother of Jesus of Nazareth.

"Jesus of Nazareth!" What volumes do these words speak! Could Nazareth wish for nobler records or a fuller history?

www.ingramcontent.com/pod-product-compliance
Lightning Source LLC
Chambersburg PA
CBHW020825230426
43666CB00007B/1106